SOCIAL REFORM AND THE REFORMATION

SOCIAL REFORM AND THE REFORMATION

BY

JACOB SALWYN SCHAPIRO, Ph.D.
Tutor in History, College of the City of New York

WIPF & STOCK · Eugene, Oregon

Wipf and Stock Publishers
199 W 8th Ave, Suite 3
Eugene, OR 97401

Social Reform and the Reformation
By Schapiro, Jacob Salwyn
ISBN 13: 978-1-60608-419-9
Publication date 01/07/2009
Previously published by Columbia University, 1909

To

PROFESSOR WILLIAM G. McGUCKIN

TEACHER AND FRIEND

PREFACE

THE Protestant movement in the sixteenth century was once easily explained, at least by the Protestants themselves. It was the struggle between the free and independent Teutonic spirit, as incarnated in Luther, with its reverence for the worth of man, against its old enemy Rome, with its oppression and corruption. Luther was the sixteenth century Arminius, Tetzel the Varus, and Wittenberg the Teutoburger Wald. The researches of the Protestant Ranke and the Catholic Janssen have brought to light an abundance of material that displays other motives besides religious ones that played a considerable part in the movement against Rome. At the end of the Middle Ages, political society was changing from feudal aristocracy to absolute monarchy. During the same time a great economic transition was taking place from agriculture to commerce. Is it possible that these three great changes in human affairs,—religious, political and economic—occurring at about the same period could have been independent of each other?

The aim of this work is to present some of the neglected economic aspects of the Lutheran Revolt. The loss of the common lands by the peasant had, perchance, as much to do with the great upheaval, now known as the Protestant Revolution, as Luther's ninety-five theses attacking indulgences. Unfortunately, the little that has hitherto been written from this point of view has come mainly from men dominated by insistent theories: for example, the Catholic Janssen, the Protestant Egelhaaf and the Socialist Bax. The field is still a new one for the investigator of critical impartiality.

I wish to thank Professor Vladimir G. Simkhovitch for suggesting the topic to me, Mr. and Miss Erb of the Columbia Library staff for their uniform kindness and courtesy, my colleague Dr. Henry Neumann and Mr. Jacob J. Shufro who performed the arduous task of revising my manuscript and Professor James T. Shotwell who aided me greatly with much valuable criticism. Above all I wish to express my deepest gratitude to Professor James Harvey Robinson to whose scholarship and suggestiveness I owe a new sense of historical values.

J. S. S.

COLLEGE OF THE CITY OF NEW YORK.
April, 1909.

ERRATA.

Page 21, fourteen lines from top, for "exports" read "imports."
Page 21, twenty lines from top, for "capital" read "money."
Page 29, two lines from bottom, for "Mexico" read "America."

CONTENTS

PART I

SOCIAL CONDITIONS IN GERMANY AT THE BEGINNING OF THE SIXTEENTH CENTURY

INTRODUCTION 15

CHAPTER I
THE GROWTH OF MONOPOLIES

The Economic Revolution in the sixteenth century 20
Its effects upon Germany 20
Germany's extraordinary prosperity 21
The Augsburg capitalists—Fuggers 23
The Welsers 23
Effect of new trade routes on the organization of business . . . 24
Revolution in prices 27
Increase of supply of the precious metals 29
Corruption of monopolies 30
Luther's attitude toward business 32
Cheating of small stock-holders 32
Investigation of monopolies by committee of the Diet of Nuremberg. 33
Defence of monopoly by city of Augsburg (1522) 34
Legislation by the Diet of Nuremberg 37
Secret alliance of merchants and princes render laws ineffectual . . 38
Corruption of government officials 39

CHAPTER II
THE INTRODUCTION OF ROMAN LAW

Legal revolution necessary because of economic and political changes 40
Influence of the canon law 42

	PAGE
Enthusiasm for the Roman law in the thirteenth century	42
Contrast between the spirit of Roman and that of German law	42
Rapid growth of study of Roman law in German Universities	43
Entrance of jurists into service of princes and into the higher territorial courts	44
Introduction of Roman law into city courts	45
The lower German courts—Their methods of procedure	46
Jurists appointed to lower courts	46
Their attitude toward German law	47
Effect of introduction of Roman law on the status of the peasants	48
Increase of legal power of the lords through control of the courts	49
Denunciation of jurists by all classes	49
The *Halbgelehrten* and legal trickery	51
Acts of the Estates of Bavaria and Würtemburg	52
Ineffectiveness of legislation against jurists	53

CHAPTER III

THE PEASANTS' REVOLT

Condition of the peasants at the end of the Middle Ages	54
The different classes of peasants	55
Dues and services	55
Complaints against the heriot	58
Economic condition of the lower nobility	59
Increases of dues and services	59
Tendency of lords to confiscate the common lands	60
The game laws	62
The entrance of capital into agriculture	63
Idealization of the peasant's life	64
The *Bundschuh* rebellions before the great revolt	65
The uprising in the Black Forest in 1525	67
The Swabian peasants organize and issue the Twelve Articles	67
The forces of the Swabian League capture Leipheim	68
The Count of Hohenlohe compelled to join the peasant league	68
The Weinsberg outrage	68
Götz von Berlichingen made commander-in-chief	69
The internal struggle in the towns	70
Florian Geyer captures Würzburg	70
The conduct of the peasants as seen by Lorenz Fries	71
Thomas Münzer and the revolt in Thuringia	71
Suppression of the revolt throughout Germany	73
Results of the uprising	73

CONTENTS

CHAPTER IV

THE ATTITUDE OF MARTIN LUTHER TOWARD THE PEASANTS' REVOLT

	PAGE
Various views of Luther's attitude toward the revolt	75
Luther's violent attack on the princes in his pamphlet, *On Secular Power*	75
Reason for this attack	75
Luther's idea as to the origin of the state	76
Complaints against him because of above pamphlet	76
His views on the relation between prince and subject	77
His denunciation of rebellion as stupid and wicked	77
Views of Melanchthon on the duty of subjects to their princes	78
Luther's idea of how reforms should be accomplished	79
His conservatism in political and economic matters; his skepticism in regard to reform	79
His contempt for the common people	80
Regarded as their champion by the peasants, who send him their Twelve Articles	80
Luther's reply in the pamphlet, *An Exhortation to Peace*	81
His views on serfdom	82
His advice to lords and peasants	83
Their refusal to heed him	84
His pamphlet, *Against the Thieving and Murderous Bands of Peasants*	84
Great reaction against Luther; his defence	86
Two explanations of his attitude	87
Real meaning of Luther's message	88

PART II

SCHEMES OF REFORM

I. The Reformation of Emperor Sigismund	93
II. The Reformation of Emperor Frederick III.	
(a) Introduction	100
(b) Text	104
III. *A New Organization of the Secular State.* By Eberlin.	
(a) Introduction	115
(b) Text	118
IV. *A Divine Evangelical Reformation.* By Hipler.	
(a) Introduction	126
(b) Text	128

		PAGE
V.	The Twelve Articles.	
	(a) Introduction	132
	(b) Text	137
VI.	*A National Constitution.* By Geismayr.	
	(a) Introduction	143
	(b) Text	147
CONCLUSION		152
GENERAL BIBLIOGRAPHY		154

PART I
SOCIAL CONDITIONS IN GERMANY AT THE BEGINNING OF THE SIXTEENTH CENTURY

INTRODUCTION

The fundamental event in the history of Europe during the sixteenth century was the partial collapse of the Mediaeval Church. The Church was the only feudalized institution which emerged triumphant from the general breakdown of feudalism in the fourteenth and fifteenth centuries. In spite of the Great Schism resulting in a loss of papal prestige in temporal matters, the vitality of the Church remained unimpaired. At the beginning of the sixteenth century it still exercised almost as much secular power as it did in the thirteenth. The priest continued to direct, judge, legislate, collect taxes, and at times, to lead in battle. The Curia Romana was still the supreme court of Europe, whose decisons few dared dispute. The pope was still recognized as the supreme head of Christendom, and his decrees both secular and religious were everywhere implicitly obeyed.

At the dawn of the sixteenth century, the Mediaeval Church found itself enveloped in the hostile atmosphere of the new learning,[1] the new politics, the new economy and the new law. It was plainly out of touch with the spirit of the times and had to give place, not necessarily to a new religion, but to a new church polity conformable to new conditions. The fact that a new set of doctrines developed with a changed relation between church and state was mainly due to the stubbornness of the

---

[1] The influence of Humanism in preparing the way for the Protestant Revolt, has no doubt been greatly exaggerated.

Church. It refused to adjust itself to the new environment by giving up its secular prerogatives. Hence the Protestant Revolution.

Luther's message meant different things to the several elements of German society that were discontented and anxious for change. To the knights, Sickingen and von Hutten, it meant the regeneration of their order and German patriotism as opposed to Italian interference. To the peasants, it meant a release from their intolerable burdens and freedom from the tyranny of their masters. From their point of view it made no difference whether the lord who overloaded them with dues, seized the common lands and oppressed them generally, was called prince, knight, bishop or abbot. The additional grudge the peasant bore the spiritual lord was due to the fact that the latter took additional taxes from him in the shape of tithes and fees. Luther had denounced the extortions and corruption of the great church officials as opposed to the Gospel. The peasant could not see why the extortions and corruption of the secular lords were any the less opposed to the Gospel; particularly as the spiritual and secular functions were often united in the same person. Even if the line of distinction between spiritual and bodily oppression was clear to a trained theologian like Luther, the common man could hardly be expected to be either able or willing to make such a distinction. As a recent writer well says:

It is easy to show, as many Lutheran Church historians have done with elaborate care, that the Reformation under Luther had nothing in common with the sudden and unexpected revolt,—as easy to prove that there was little in common between the "Spiritual Poverty" of Francis of Assisi and the vulgar communism of the "Brethren and the Sisters of the

Free Spirit," between the doctrines of Wiclif and the gigantic labor strike headed by Watt Tyler and Priest Ball, between the teaching of Hus and the extreme Taborite fanatics. But the fact remains that the voice of Luther awoke echoes he never dreamt of and that its effects cannot be measured by changes in doctrine, or by a reformation in ecclesiastical organization. The times of the Reformation were ripe for revolution, and the words of the bold preacher, coming when all men were restless and most men were oppressed, appealing especially to those who felt the burden heavy and the yoke galling, were followed by high-sounding reverberations.[1]

The great economic changes of the sixteenth century, the discovery of new routes to India and of the New World, the increase in the supply of precious metals and the creation of a world market, were bringing about a vast change in the internal affairs of Germany. Commercial methods were revolutionized. The organization of great trading companies with sufficient capital to cope with the new problems presented by an international trade became inevitable. To these commercial syndicates were attributed many of the evils of the day: high prices, scarcity of money, the adulteration of foods and the corruption of officials charged with the duty of enforcing the laws against monopoly. The capitalists were also accused of ruining the small free-hold farmer, by advancing him money on his land at usurious rates of interest and then foreclosing the mortgage when he could not pay. The small merchant being unable to compete with the companies, was either forced out of business entirely or compelled to buy his goods from them.

The rise of new commercial interests and the growth of princely absolutism at the expense of the central imperial

[1] Lindsay, *A History of the Reformation*, i, p. 327.

authority found a necessary expression in the introduction of Roman law. The application of Roman principles of jurisprudence to German conditions had the effect of uprooting old customs and traditions. The jurists, having absorbed the strict notions of individual possession contained in the ancient code, became the uncompromising enemies of the old communal ideals of the German people. Their legal technicalities were a mystery to the simple-minded who saw in them merely devilish trickery for the purpose of depriving the freeholder of his farm and the village of its common lands. The lawyers formed a special class in the employ of princes and companies and were consequently hated by all classes, who denounced them as unscrupulous tools of tyranny and monopoly.

The rapid transformation that Germany was undergoing at the end of the Middle Ages was sure to find expression in the popular literature of the period. Mediaeval society was profoundly agitated by the changes that were taking place in the economic, political and religious life of the people. Hence schemes of reform, from the most moderate to the most revolutionary, from the most local to the most universal, became the order of the day. Every change, whether for better or for worse, brought discontent which soon found voice in a "reformation" or a set of "articles." The six programs of reform reproduced in Part II are but examples of many others of the same kind. The variety of these plans and their widely different origin show plainly that other thoughts besides those purely religious were occupying the minds of the people in Luther's day.

The political chaos of Germany caused many to look to the emperor as the only one to restore order and justice. The old Prester John legend[1] of a conquering hero-king from the East who would come to establish universal peace, right all wrongs and so prepare the way for the Kingdom of Christ upon earth, took a powerful hold on the imagination of the time. The imaginary constitutions fathered upon the Emperors Sigismund and Frederick III, although they were doubtless forgeries, were nevertheless expressions of real popular sentiments. They became the arsenal from which were drawn the most powerful weapons of invective and argument during the great Peasants' Revolt. The Reformation of Emperor Sigismund and the Reformation of Emperor Frederick III belong to the type of vague emotional radicalism, characteristic of documents that are mainly "protests." The plans of Eberlin and Geismayr are "schemes," ready-made, Utopian and visionary. They bear the earmarks of having sprung full-grown from the brains of individuals and not in response to any organized demand. The Twelve Articles and Hipler's manifesto, especially the former, may be described as "demands," being fairly representative of a definite class, having definite grievances and seeking definite remedies.

[1] Bezold, *Geschichte der deut. Reformation*, p. 148.

CHAPTER I

THE GROWTH OF MONOPOLIES

THE economic revolution of the sixteenth century was not industrial but commercial. The rapid expansion of trade from the petty inter-town business of the Middle Ages to the world commerce of the sixteenth century, resulting in the creation of a world market, was caused mainly by a change of trade routes due to the voyages and discoveries of the Portugese navigators like Bartholomew Diaz and Vasco da Gama.[1] The result of finding an all-water route to India was the shifting of trade from the Mediterranean to the Atlantic. The geographic position of Germany in the middle of Europe had proved exceedingly advantageous as it made her the center of a great international commerce with Italy on one side and with the Hanseatic towns on the other. But the new world-commerce was inevitably bound to cause great changes in German trade and markets.

Up to the sixteenth century there was considerable trade between South Germany and Italy. To the "Fondaco dei Tedeschi" in Venice, a great German emporium, came the German merchants or their representatives, who purchased vast quantities of spices, silks, precious stones, metals, fruits, etc., brought from the East by Italian ships. But the geographical discoveries had the effect of causing Lisbon and Antwerp to displace Venice and

[1] Another reason was the increased use of the precious metals due to a larger output of German mines and importation from America.

Genoa as the European centers of Asiatic trade. The German merchants were not slow to take advantage of this change. In 1503 the great firm of Welser of Augsburg, together with other merchants, established warehouses in Lisbon where they got special privileges from the king of Portugal, Don Emanuel. They were given the right to participate in trading expeditions, to import from India free of duty, to use Portugese ships and to have their own courts.[1]

Yet all this increase of trade meant no corresponding increase of production. The methods and organization of industry in vogue at the close of the Middle Ages were the same as in the thirteenth century. Hence the vast trade consisted of exports only, and in exchange Germany sent not her own products but her precious metals. This was made possible by the increased output of German and Austrian silver mines and by the importation of precious metals from America.[2] The rise of a world market made possible for the first time the productive employment of capital. In the Middle Ages capital had been used chiefly in defraying the expenses of military expeditions, paying ransoms and buying armor, weapons or jewels. It was seldom or never applied to land or industry as a form of investment.

The end of the fifteenth century witnessed Germany's high-noon of prosperity. Old and insignificant towns like Augsburg, Nuremberg and Ulm blossomed forth into wealthy and populous cities. The great merchants vied with princes and kings in magnificence and luxury. Their gardens, palaces and entertainments were the envy of the poorer nobility. Aeneas Sylvius, writing in 1458,

[1] Janssen, *Geschichte des deutschen Volks*, i, p. 434.
[2] *Cf. infra*, p. 30. As production was not organized, little money was invested in machinery and other forms of fixed capital.

says: "We proclaim it aloud, Germany has never been richer or more prosperous than to-day. She takes the lead of all other nations in wealth and power. One can say truly that God has favored this land above all others. On all sides are seen cultivated farms, cornfields and vineyards and gardens. Everywhere are great buildings, walled cities and well-to-do farmers."[1] Jacob Wimpheling, the famous humanist, declared fifty years later that "Germany was never more prosperous than to-day, and she owes it chiefly to the untiring industry and energy of her people, artisans as well as merchants. The peasants too are rich and prosperous."[2] The desire for wealth became the all-absorbing passion, and we find the popular preacher Martin Butzer denouncing the materialistic spirit of the time. "All the world," he says, "is running after those trades and occupations that will bring the most gain. The study of the arts and sciences is set aside for the basest kind of manual work. All the clever heads, which have been endowed by God with capacity for the nobler studies are engrossed by commerce, which nowadays is so saturated with dishonesty that it is the last sort of business an honorable man ought to engage in."[3]

The headquarters of German capitalism was the city of Augsburg which, because of its situation, acted as a distributing center for all Eastern goods received from both Lisbon and Venice. The two greatest trading houses of Augsburg were the Fuggers and Welsers. The great Fugger family began as merchants but very soon turned to mining and banking. Jacob Fugger got control of nearly all the copper mines of Hungary, Tyrol, Carinthia and Thuringia, through advancing loans to the authori-

---

[1] Janssen, i, p. 436.   [2] *Ibid.*, i, p. 438.   [3] *Ibid.*, ii, p. 456.

THE GROWTH OF MONOPOLIES

ties. The collection of taxes was uncertain, irregular and unsystematic, and the emperor and princes were frequently forced to rely upon the Fuggers for large loans for which in return they granted them extensive mining privileges or gave them lands and castles.[1] The Fuggers were the Rothschilds of their day and had important interests all over the world. At one time they were considered worth sixty-three millions of florins.[2] The organization of this great concern was largely a family affair. The sons, sons-in-law or nephews at first became the "factors" or agents in the numerous branches and later were made full members and stockholders.

The Welsers, on the contrary, were little interested in banking or mining but were almost entirely devoted to the importation of Eastern goods. Their headquarters were at Augsburg but much of the business was done through the branches or warehouses, which were established in Lisbon, Nuremberg, Antwerp, Dantzig, Venice, Milan, Rome, Genoa, Berne, Zurich, Lyons and Saragossa. Unlike the Fuggers, the organization of the Welser firm was not in the hands of one family but was administered by many stockholders, who took charge of the factories in the various cities and shared in the profits.[3]

---

[1] In 1507 Emperor Maximilian pawned the county of Kirschberg and the manor of Weissenhorn to the Fuggers in return for a loan of 50,000 florins. In 1509 he negotiated another loan of 170,000 ducats; in 1514 another of 44,000 florins, and in 1516 another of 20,000 florins. Ehrenberg, *Das Zeitalter der Fugger*, i, pp. 95-97.

[2] Conrad Meyer, secretary of the firm, declared that "the capital of the Fuggers received an increase of 13,000,000 florins in the course of seven years." Greiff, *Lucas Rem*, p. 94; Janssen, i, p. 473.

[3] Greiff, 19. The exploitation of lands in America was at one time the ambition of the Welsers. In return for a loan, the emperor granted them Venezuela as a hereditary fief on the following conditions: (1)

In spite of mediaeval hindrances,—robber knights, strand laws, tolls, laws against interest and usury—business developed at a startling rate, largely because of the inducement of enormous profits.[1] Those who assumed large risks often reaped unusual rewards. In 1504 an association of Augsburg and Nuremberg capitalists headed by the Welsers fitted out three ships at an expense of 66,000 ducats and sent them along with the Portuguese convoy to the Indies. In four years they returned loaded with spices, drugs, precious stones and other costly goods out of which the merchants made a clear profit of 175 per cent.[2]

The change of trade routes soon produced a radical effect on the organization of business. Formerly the individual German merchant journeyed to nearby Venice for his goods. The small dealer could easily compete with the large one, as the expense of transportation was proportionately the same. It was quite a different matter however, when far-away Lisbon became the depot for Eastern wares. The cost of transportation became so

they must build two cities and two forts within two years; (2) they must transport 300 Spaniards and 50 master-miners to work the silver mines. This enterprise proved a failure and was afterwards abandoned. B. Moses, *The Establishment of Spanish Rule in America*, p. 163.

[1] The capital of the Fuggers rose from 196,761 gulden in 1511 to 2,021,202 gulden in 1527, and yielded a yearly profit of 54½ per cent. on the investment. Greiff, p. 30; Ehrenberg, i, p. 196; pp. 388 *et seq.* The Hochstätters with an investment of 900 gulden earned 33,000 gulden in six years. Janssen, i, p. 472. Albrecht Scheuerl of Nuremberg, a dealer in spices, copper, satins and jewelry, during the years 1449-1461, averaged 25 per cent net profit yearly. Ehrenberg, i, p. 390. "An investment of 500 gulden would bring in seven years a return of 24,500 gulden. Many small people began to invest their money, and when the Hochstätters failed, the number of people ruined was great." Bezold, p. 34.

[2] Falke, *Die Geschichte des deutschen Handels*, ii, p. 20; A. Beer, *Allgemeine Geschichte des Welthandel*, ii, p. 419.

great that agencies had to be established there for the purpose of consolidating shipments. These agents being on the spot, could also take advantage of any changes in the market. Moreover, the king of Portugal demanded a share of the profits of all trading expeditions under his protection. All this necessitated the employment of a larger capital than the ordinary German trader possessed in order to make an undertaking profitable at all. The wealthier merchants quickly took advantage of this condition and organized themselves into associations or "companies." At first they united merely for the purpose of buying and transporting in common in order to reduce expenses; but very soon they united for the purpose of selling as well. These associations quickly developed into monopolistic combines that controlled the entire Asiatic trade in Germany and arbitrarily fixed the prices of all Eastern articles. The small merchant found himself crowded to the wall. All methods familiar to monopoly everywhere and at all times were used to drive him out of business. Luther complains in his pamphlet *On Trade and Usury*, printed in 1524:

The monopolists succeed in driving out the small merchants by buying up large quantities of goods, and then suddenly raise the prices when they are left masters of the field. So, these monopolists, have everything in their hands and do whatever they wish, raise and lower prices at will and oppress and ruin small dealers, just as a great pike swallows up a lot of little fishes. They have become lords over God's creatures and free from all bonds of religion and humanity . . . . . If monopolies are permitted to exist, then justice and righteousness must vanish.[1]

[1] Luther, *Werke* (Weimar), xv, pp. 312–313.

Lucas Rem, the merchant chronicler of Augsburg, writes of Hochstätter of his city:

He had the reputation of being a good Christian, yet he often oppressed the common man. He would buy up at good bargains all the ash-wood, corn and wine, and keep them in storage till a great demand arose for them when he would sell at very high prices. Often he would buy up all of a certain kind of goods at a price above the market, and thus create a demand for the article and sell at his own price. No merchant worth less than 100,000 florins could compete with him.[1]

The Diet of Nuremberg complained in 1522:

The companies take special care to monopolize those spices that are most needed. If one company is not rich enough it associates itself with another and so gets the article in its hands. If a poor merchant desires to deal in these wares, the companies are immediately at his throat. They are able to ruin him, because having more money and more goods, they are able to sell cheaper and give longer credit. . . . The companies are responsible for lessened business. To-day, there is one great concern with many branches where formerly there were twenty independent merchants. The companies do their business largely by correspondence with their agents, hence the roads bring in fewer tolls and the government receives less dues. . . . Furthermore, our good gold and silver money is sent out of the land . . . therefore in many towns there are risings of the common man, which will spread more and more.[2]

The Landtag of the Austrian hereditary dominions at Innsbruck in 1518 declared:

The great companies have monopolized all things and are not

---

[1] Greiff, pp. 95-96, quoted by Janssen, i, p. 474. For other instances see Ehrenberg, i, pp. 214, 398.

[2] *Deutsche Reichstagsakten*, iii, pp. 581 *et seq.*

to be borne any longer. All sorts of merchandise—silver, copper, steel, iron, linen, sugar, spices, corn, cattle, wine, meat, tallow and leather—have fallen into their hands. Through their money power, they have become so strong, that no merchant having less than 10,000 florins is able to compete with them. They raise prices arbitrarily when it is to their advantage and as a result their incomes are as great as those of princes. They are a great harm to our land.[1]

The Eastern trade gave the first impulse to monopoly because of the comparative ease in controlling the supply. But soon domestic goods, too, fell under the control of the companies. The companies were able to force down the buying price by being in a position to purchase vast quantities of commodities at one time. Taking advantage of having ready money, they would buy up fields of crops in the stalk at low prices by advancing money to the peasants. Through their completely developed and widespread organization, the companies were always well-informed on the state of the market. Through their agents they were informed when and where there was a bad crop and took advantage of this information to advance prices.

During the first quarter of the sixteenth century there occurred a most remarkable revolution in prices. Every article, foreign and domestic, rose enormously, in some cases one hundred per cent and over.[2] Naturally the

[1] Falke, ii, p. 338.

[2] Between 1475 and 1500 there had been a fall in the prices of farm products; grain and wheat fell 20 per cent; oats and rye 25 per cent; cattle 22 per cent. Lamprecht, *Deutsches Wirtschaftsleben im Mittelalter*, i, pp. 621 *et seq*. From 1500-1525 there was a remarkable rise. Beef rose 15 per cent; pork 50 per cent; clothing 50 per cent; herring from ⅓ pfennig to 20 pfennig a piece; codfish from 9 pfennig to 12 pfennig a pound; rye from 1 schilling to 7 schillings a measure; wheat from 2½ schillings to 7 schillings a measure; oats from 16½ pfennig to 36 pfennig

monopolies were blamed by all classes for this extraordinary advance in the prices of the necessities of life. The report of the "Committee on Monopolies" appointed by the Diet of Nuremberg in 1523 accuses the companies of making a secret agreement with the king of Portugal to give them rebates in order to enable them to control the market and raise prices:

No matter how high the prices are which the king of Portugal asks of the companies, it pays both them and him, for it is agreed that the king shall sell to no other merchant except for a still higher price. For example, he gets from 18 to 20 ducats for a cwt. of pepper on condition that he charge others 24 ducats a cwt. Such methods cause a general rise of prices of all spices. The companies do not raise prices on all things at one time, but one year one article, next year another article, etc.; now it is the price of saffron that goes up, now of cloves, then of pepper, etc. By such methods they avoid arousing suspicion.[1]

a measure; butter from 5 pfennig to 10 pfennig a pound; salt from 16 pfennig to 26 pfennig a measure; shoes from 24 pfennig to 54 pfennig a pair. L. Keller, "Zur Geschichte der Preisbewegung in Deutschland während, 1466-1525," in *Jahrbücher für Nationalökonomie und Statistik*, vol. xxxiv.

In the Bishopric of Münster from 1501 to 1530, farm products rose 25 per cent; wine, 20 per cent; animals and animal products, 30 per cent; salt, 15 per cent; honey, 5 per cent; and spices, 100 per cent. Wiebe, *Zur Geschichte der Preisrevolution des 16 und 17 Jahrhunderts*, p. 381. In Würtemburg, wine rose 49 per cent; wheat, 32 per cent. Janssen, i, p. 470. The rise in prices of all sorts of spices was even more startling. The Select Committee on Monopolies appointed by the Diet of Nuremberg reported that the best saffron in 1516 cost 3 gr. 6 kr.; in 1522 cost 4 gr. 15 kr.; medium saffron in 1519 cost 2 gr. 21 kr.; in 1522, 4 gr.; cloves in 1512 cost 19 shillings; in 1522 they cost 2 gr.; stick cinnamon in 1516 cost 1 gr. 18 kr.; in 1518 they cost 2 gr. 3 kr.; nutmeg in 1519 cost 27 kr.; in 1522, 3 gr. 28 kr.; best pepper in 1518 cost 18 kr.; in 1522, 32 kr.; ginger in 1516 cost 22 kr.; in 1517, 1 gr. 3 kr.; sugar in 1516, 11 gr.; in 1518, 20 gr. *Deutsche Reichstagsakten*, iii, p. 576; Ranke, *Hist. of Ger. during the Reformation*, ii, p. 49.

[1] *Deutsche Reichstagsakten*, iii, p. 575.

THE GROWTH OF MONOPOLIES

The nobility, in a complaint to the Diet of Nuremberg issued in 1523, say:

It is well known that a German company made an agreement with the king of Portugal to buy 600,000 gulden worth of pepper with the condition that a higher price should be charged to other German merchants. . . . In this way they tax every inhabitant and oppress the common man. . . For every investment of 100 gulden, they get in one year 40, 50, 60 and even 80 gulden profit. In one year they steal more than all the thieves in our land do in ten; and moreover they are not called robbers but honorable men.[1]

The existence of monopolies was not the only cause for the phenomenal rise of prices during the years 1500-1525. Other causes operated as well, such as the increase in demand due to the growth of prosperity, the decrease for a time in the supply from Venice owing to the war in which the latter was engaged with the League of Cambray, and more particularly to the increased supply of precious metals which swelled the volume of currency in circulation. The yearly output of the silver and copper mines of Germany and Hungary increased enormously. Moreover a new source of supply was opened in America which was later to become the main reliance of the Old World. The silver mines of Mexico were beginning to be worked by the Spaniards and the ore shipped to Europe.[2]

[1] Falke, ii, p. 339.
[2] The silver mines of the Erzgebirge in 1471 were the richest in Germany. During the first thirty years of their operation they yielded 352,000 quintals of ore. The silver mines of Annaberg during 1496-1499 netted a profit of 125,000 thalers. The mines of Mansfeld were considered inexhaustible in silver and copper. In poor years they yielded from 8,000 to 15,000 quintals. The Bohemian and Tyrolian mines yielded great quantities of gold and silver. The Fuggers derived a yearly income of 200,000 gulden from their mines in the Tyrol. The Hochstätters, between 1511 and 1517 produced 149,777 mark silver

Nevertheless there was a general belief that monopoly was solely responsible for the prevailing high prices. This was voiced by Luther in his treatise, *On Trade and Usury*, issued in 1524. Here we read:

The merchants complain of robber-nobles, who attack, rob and imprison them. If these merchants suffer because of their righteousness they are indeed saints . . . yet great evil and unchristian robbery results throughout the world because of the activity of the merchants. It is no wonder then that God punishes them; as what they gain by robbery they lose through robbery.[1]

The popular preacher Geiler von Keiserberg denounced the monopolists

as greater extortioners than the Jews . . . who plunder not only foreign wares with which we could dispense but also the very necessaries of life, as corn, meat and wine. Prices they raise to suit their greed and they feast on the fruits of the hard labor of the poor. . . . Such people should be driven out like wolves, since they fear neither God nor man and breed famine, thirst and poverty.[2]

The greater luxury of the wealthy merchants caused many to complain that the monopolies were destroying simple life and making it impossible for a man of small means to get along. "In a short time," writes Luther, "because of usury and avarice, he that could formerly

and 52,915 cwt. of copper. Greiff, p. 94; Mosch, *Geschichte des Bergbaus in Deutschland*, ii, p. 223, quoted by Janssen, i, p. 471.

The early output of the American mines was not very great; nevertheless, it must have had some influence on prices in Europe. From 1493 to 1500 they yielded 250,000 pesos silver yearly; from 1500 to 1545 it increased to 3,000,000 pesos per year. E. G. Bourne, *Spain in America*, p. 301.

[1] *Werke* (Weimar), xv, p. 311.   [2] Janssen, i, p. 467.

live on 100 gulden cannot do so now on 200."[1] The strongest protest came from the lower nobility or knights who, poor and jealous of the rich burghers, had special reasons for favoring the simple life. In a celebrated dialogue called *Praedones* or "The Robbers," Ulrich von Hutten, the spokesman of this class, declares that there are four classes of robbers: merchants, jurists, priests and knights, and the greatest robbers of them all are the merchants.[2] Complaints were also made that the companies were depleting Germany of her gold and silver coins to buy worthless luxuries. Luther declared that "our good money goes to buy silks and satins from India which are of no use to us. . . . In this way we make everybody else rich and remain beggars ourselves."[3]

The extraordinary development of commercialism brought along with it all those evils which usually accompany such a change. The pamphlets of the time abound in denunciations of wholesale adulteration of goods, especially foods.[4] The Landtag of the Austrian hereditary dominions held at Innsbruck in 1518 complains that the monopolists "adulterate the spices they import; to ginger they add brick-dust and mix unhealthy stuff with their pepper."[5] Luther declared in his pamphlet *On Trade and Usury* that the companies

have learned the trick of placing such spices as pepper, ginger and saffron in damp vaults in order to increase their weight. There is not a single article out of which they can't make an

---

[1] *Werke* (Walch), x, p. 1084.
[2] Böcking, *Ulrichs von Huttens Schriften*, iv, pp. 363 *et seq.*
[3] *Werke* (Walch), x, p. 392.
[4] For examples see Baur, *Deutschland in dem Jahren 1517-1525*, pp. 123 *et seq.*, and Hagen, *Deutschl. lit. und relig. Verhältnisse*, ii, pp. 323 *et seq.*
[5] Falke, ii, p. 339.

unfair profit through false measuring, counting or weighing, or by producing artificial colors. They put the good quality on top and bottom and the bad in the middle. There is no end to their trickery and no tradesman will trust another, for they know one another's ways.[1]

Luther's general conception of business smacked of the mediaeval. His suspicious attitude toward capital led him to regard interest in the light of usury, particularly when he saw fortunes made quickly without any visible labor at the plow or loom. "How can it be possible," he exclaims, "that anyone can through righteous methods in a short time become richer than kings and emperors! . . . Is it any wonder that the monopolists are becoming kings and we beggars!"[2] The principle of business he declared, is to sell as dearly as possible, which is against Christian notions, for it resembles robbery. Credit is foolish as well as wicked. Business violates the foundation of Christian ethics and ought to be limited. "Those who sell for as high a price as they wish, who take or give credit, are the sources of all sorts of wide-spreading wickedness and trickery."[3]

The cheating of the smaller stockholder by those who controlled the management of the companies was not unknown. In 1498 a syndicate of Augsburg capitalists planned to control the copper market at Venice. It was easy for them to do so as they owned most of the Hungarian and Tyrolian mines which supplied the Venetian market. The syndicate was organized in a period of over-production and falling prices. The Fuggers, who had led in its organization, by secretly underbidding their associates, drove them out of the market and so gained

[1] *Werke* (Weimar), xv, p. 311.
[2] *Ibid.*, p. 312.
[3] *Ibid.*, p. 304.

complete control.[1] Managers and directors were accused of dishonesty in keeping accounts. An Augsburg chronicle of 1512 states that "the merchants form great companies and become wealthy, but many of them are dishonest and cheat one another. Hence the directors of the companies who have charge of the accounts are nearly always richer than their associates. Those who thus grew rich are clever, since they do not have the reputation of being thieves."[2]

The agitation against the companies became so great that it finally reached the point of legislation. The Diet of Cologne in 1512 took up the matter for the first time with a view to governmental action. In a resolution they declared:

In a short time, great trading companies have risen that deal in all sorts of wares and control prices and terms for their own benefit. As they inflict much injury upon all classes in the empire by their dishonorable dealings, so we declare, that for the sake of the commonweal, all such injurious traffic be forbidden. Anyone found guilty of disobeying this ordinance shall have his property confiscated by the magistrates of his town. In case the latter refuse to do their duty then the imperial authorities shall take action instead.[3]

This decree was enforced by neither the local nor the imperial authorities. The question of monopoly came up again in a more aggravated form at the great Diet of Nuremberg in 1522. A committee was appointed by the diet to investigate the whole matter and to recommend legislation. The committee in order to get full information on the subject sent a questionnaire to the councils of the towns that represented the trading inter-

[1] Ehrenberg, i, p. 397.   [2] Janssen, i, p. 473.
[3] *Deutsche Reichstagsakten*, iii, p. 574.

ests. They were asked to give their opinion: (1) whether the monopolies are useful or hurtful to the empire; (2) whether it were better to destroy or regulate the merchant associations; and (3) what methods should be employed to accomplish the end desired. Answers were received from the city councils of Ulm, Frankfort and Augsburg. The reply of Ulm was: (1) that monopolies were an evil; (2) that it would, however, be unwise to destroy them, but better to limit the membership of any merchant company to a father, his son and his son-in-law; and (3) that to accomplish this a heavy tax should be laid on all imported articles.[1]

The reply of the city of Augsburg is very long, but it contains so interesting a defense of monopoly that it is worth quoting:

Christendom (or shall we say the whole world?), is rich because of business. If the spice trade were taken away from the king of Portugal he would consider it as great a calamity as war. Such is the importance of business. Florence is a great and mighty city solely because of business. Likewise Milan, whose commerce was developed through the foresight of Galeazzo Sforza. . . . Consider the wealth of Portugal and Spain, all built up through trade. Where there is no business the country is of little account. Hence it follows that commerce is useful to kings and princes, and good for the common weal. The more business a country does, the more prosperous are its people. There are lands where business interests are better protected than in Germany and where they do everything to encourage and attract the merchants. . . . Commerce adds to the coffers of princes and is besides absolutely essential to the common welfare; where there are many merchants there is plenty of work. Only the great

[1] *Deutsche Reichstagsakten*, iii, pp. 554-558. The reply of the city of Frankfort is not found in this collection.

merchants are able to do business on a large scale because the small traders have not enough capital. Stupid people go around and say that the companies carry on their business largely through correspondence and hence escape paying the tolls which are borne by the small merchant. This is untrue, as the companies have to pay tolls on wagonful and shipful.

The reply goes on to say that if the Germans do not want any spices, the companies are perfectly willing to send them elsewhere; but that this would result in a loss of revenue to the princes:

It is impossible to limit the size of the companies, for that would limit business and hurt the common welfare; the bigger and more numerous they are the better for everybody. If a merchant is not perfectly free to do business in Germany he will go elsewhere to Germany's loss. Any one can see what harm and evil such an action would mean to us. If a merchant cannot do business, above a certain amount, what is he to do with his surplus money? It is impossible to set a limit to business and it would be well to let the merchant alone and put no restrictions on his ability or capital. . . . Some people talk of limiting the earning capacity of investments. This would be unbearable and would work great injustice and harm by taking away the livelihood of widows, orphans and other sufferers, noble and non-noble, who derive their income from investments in these companies. Many merchants out of love and friendship invest the money of their friends—men, women and children—who know nothing of business, in order to provide them with an assured income. Hence any one can see that the idea that the merchant companies undermine the public welfare ought not to be seriously considered. The small merchant complains that he can not earn as much as the companies. That is like the old complaint of the common laborer that he earns so little wages. All this is true enough, but are the complaints justifiable?

The report goes on to prove that very often the companies help out the small merchants, through credit and loans and so enable them to rise in business and become rich. "How then can one say that the rich trample down the poor when they actually save them from their own incompetence or misfortunes?" In answer to the charge of corruption the report declares that there are a few bad companies who adulterate their wares and monopolize certain articles; but why, because of these exceptions, should the business interests of Germany be attacked? It closes with a threat that if action is taken against them the trading companies will leave Germany.[1]

The report of the investigation committee to the Diet showed a determination to get rid of the monopolistic features of the trading companies, yet was tempered with a cautious desire not to injure business. It really proposed to regulate, not to destroy, the great merchant associations. "The government has not done its duty" (in not enforcing the decree of the Diet of Cologne), reads the report, "and yet at the same time small thieves have been punished severely. The companies have done more injury to the common man than all the highwaymen and thieves put together; yet the monopolists and their associates strut about in all the magnificence and luxury that wealth can buy."[2] After quoting instances of the rise of prices and roundly denouncing the evil methods and aims of the companies, the report goes on to say:

We have already given reasons why the great companies should be destroyed, but that does not mean that all business associations should be done away with. Such a course would be foolish and harmful to the whole German people, for the fol-

[1] *Deutsche Reichstagsakten*, iii, pp. 562 *et seq.*   [2] *Ibid.*, p. 573.

lowing reasons: In the first place, it would give the foreigners an opportunity to take over our business and then the companies could exploit Germany at will. Secondly, if we permitted only single individuals to trade, failure would be sure to result, which would be avoided by permitting associations of moderate size only. This, too, would give an opportunity to an individual who possesses great capital to do exactly what a company does and yet be within the law. Finally, a single individual cannot go to many places for goods, and he cannot afford to hire agents, as this costs money. Therefore the foreign companies will have a great advantage over the German merchant.[1]

After a great deal of debate, the Diet passed a series of laws designed to mitigate the evils of monopoly. These provide that:

I. Companies are not to be capitalized for more than fifty thousand gulden and are to have only three branches. A statement of its membership and business must be filed with the government.

II. The profits must be divided every two years and the authorities notified of the fact.

III. No money may be loaned at usurious rates of interest.

IV. No commodity shall be entirely under one control.

V. No merchant shall buy during a single quarter of a year more than 100 cwt. of pepper, 100 cwt. of ginger and 50 cwt. of other spices.

VI. The companies shall not impose a minimum selling price.

VII. The government shall regulate the prices of wares because the companies secretly agree to raise prices.

VIII. Each article imported shall be taxed by the imperial government a fixed sum on the hundredweight.

[1] *Deutsche Reichstagsakten*, iii, p. 582.

IX. Voyaging to Portugal is to be forbidden because of too much speculation there, and the king of that country is to be asked to send the spices into Germany.

X. The penalty for violating these laws is to be confiscation of the property of the company, one-half to go to the imperial and the other half to the local government.[1]

In spite of the denunciations, petitions, laws and decrees, the monopolies were not seriously disturbed. The vast wealth of the great companies, the political importance of the cities which they controlled, the weakness of the central government and the intimate relations of the merchants with the governing powers, were proof against all laws aimed at them. The decrees of the Diet of Nuremberg very soon became a dead letter. The scheme to tax all imports for the benefit of the imperial treasury would have enhanced the power of the central government, to which all elements represented in the Diet were strongly opposed. The merchants immediately sent a strong protest to the Emperor Charles V against this tariff, declaring that business would not be able to stand it and intimating that they would find a way to avoid paying the tax in case he refused to heed their protest.[2]

The city magistrates and princes secretly shared in the profits of the monopolies. Many of the town councilors were themselves members of the trading companies; even the imperial officers were often bribed with presents of shares of stock.[3] The Diet of Worms declared in 1521 that "it is reasonably presumed that persons of influence

[1] *Deutsche Reichstagsakten*, iii, pp. 582–599.
[2] Schmoller, *Zur Geschichte der national-ökonomischen Ansichten in Deutschland während der Reformationsperiode*, p. 649.
[3] *Ibid.*, p. 500.

in the empire, like princes, electors and councilors, share in the profits of the companies; hence oppression becomes all the heavier."[1] "I hear," exclaims Luther, "that the princes have a finger in the pie and have become the companions of thieves. The princes readily hang a thief who steals a gulden but are hail-fellows-well-met with those who rob the whole world; hence the proverb 'the big thieves hang the little ones.'"[2]

The agitation against monopoly, ostensibly in the interest of the "common man," was really in the interest of the small dealer who had just enough influence to make his complaint heard but not enough to compel effective action. Shut out from the Portuguese market, he was forced to buy his wares from the very companies who were driving him out of business.

[1] Kluckhohn, *Zur Gesch. der Handelsgesellschaften u. Monopole*, p. 672.
[2] *Werke* (Weimar), xv, p. 313.

CHAPTER II

THE INTRODUCTION OF THE ROMAN LAW INTO GERMANY

THE great economic changes of the sixteenth century, from natural to money economy, from agriculture to commerce, were sure to find legal expression in the jurisprudence of the empire. The old Teutonic law, comprehending only an agrarian state of society, found itself suddenly confronted for the first time by a host of problems dealing with credit, obligations, contracts, etc., which were so far out of its range and spirit that a legal revolution was necessary.

The old German law was a vast array of uncodified local laws and customs, varying with the principality, commune, town, village or manor. It was weak, loose and provincial; it lacked entirely a common legal basis or set of principles which would hold good everywhere in the empire, and was rightly called the *jus incertum*.[1] The new economy demanded uniformity and precision, and the highly-developed and comprehensive system of Roman law which was ready at hand, suited it admirably. "Conditions had changed and law was taken to fit them

---

[1] Attempts were made in the fourteenth and fifteenth centuries to codify the German laws. Johann von Freiberg in the fourteenth century published his *Summa ex Decretalibus*, a collection of old German laws with interpretations according to Roman principles of jurisprudence. It passed through several editions, but never became sufficiently important to forestall the introduction of Roman law. Stobbe, *Geschichte der deutschen Rechtsquellen*, i, p. 636.

wherever found and without very great scruple about its foreign form and character."[1]

The political changes were no less significant than the economic in forwarding the adoption of a foreign code. The essential political phenomenon of Germany in the fifteenth and sixteenth centuries was a tendency towards princely centralization, at the expense of the empire on the one hand and of the lower nobility on the other. Great princes, like the elector of Saxony, the margrave of Brandenburg, the dukes of Bavaria and Würtemburg and the archbishop of Cologne, had risen to a height of power that made them practically the heads of independent states. The development of the absolutism of the princes, vassals of the emperor, was along the line of least resistance, as the princely states were vital political organisms, whereas the empire was but a shadow. The knights, impoverished by high prices and the fall of land values, their fighting status made lower by gunpowder, rose in rebellion under the gallant Franz von Sickingen. But all in vain. The revolt was sternly suppressed by the archbishop of Treves, and the importance of the knights, the most romantic figures of the Middle Ages, was gone never to return.

The princes counted on the assistance of the Roman jurists to legitimize what they had accomplished by force. The Roman lawyers freely applied the familiar dictum of Roman law, "quod principi placuit, legis habet vigorem," in upholding their patrons in legal contentions. Jacob Wimpheling complains that "according to the abomina-

[1] Eichhorn, *Deutsche Staats- und Rechtsgeschichte*, i, p. 246. It should be borne in mind that the political disintegration of Germany made practically impossible the development of a new common law, national in scope and character, either by central judicial decisions, as in England, or by legislation.

ble axioms of the jurists the princes must be everything in the land and the people nothing. The people are of use only to obey, to serve and to pay taxes."[1] Moreover, the spirit of German law differed widely from that of the Roman. German law took into consideration the class, calling and condition of the litigants, and contained special provisions to suit each. The Roman legal system, on the contrary, recognized but one master, the prince; one servant, the subjects; and one law for all, high or low, rich or poor.[2]

The study of canon law prepared the way for the introduction of the Roman code. The former resembled the latter in method of procedure, though it differed from it radically in the spirit of interpretation. The use of canon law was general in the church courts throughout the Middle Ages. The popes, it must be remembered, however, were strongly opposed to the introduction of the civil code, particularly in non-Latin countries. In 1219 Pope Honorius III forbade the study of Roman law at the University of Paris on pain of excommunication. In 1254 Innocent IV extended the decree to include all countries except Italy.[3]

During the twelfth and thirteenth centuries many students, Germans in particular, owing to the connection between Italy and Germany, thronged the law university at Bologna. They returned full of enthusiasm for Roman law and contempt for the German. They were infatuated with its logical reasoning, subtle distinctions and comprehensive principles. They considered the Roman code

[1] Janssen, i, p. 571.
[2] Jhring, *Geist des römischen Rechts*, ii, p. 99.
[3] Schmidt, *Die Reception des römischen Rechts in Deutschland*, pp. 107-128. Perhaps one of the reasons for this attitude of the popes was that they wanted Italy to have a monopoly of the teaching of Roman law.

as the only system suitable to all nations and at all times.[1] At first this new tendency was purely an intellectual movement, as there was little opportunity to apply it in practice, since the private law was as yet entirely German. The new study received hearty encouragement at the hands of the emperors, particularly Frederick I and II, because it favored their claims as against those of the popes with whom they were then struggling;[2] but it was not till the middle of the fifteenth century that it was introduced into German universities. Here it made rapid progress, doubling and tripling each year the number of its students and professors.[3]

Long before the Roman jurists had forced their way into the courts, their services were in demand as notaries, private secretaries, councilors and ambassadors of the emperors and princes. They very quickly displaced the clergy in these offices. The jurists would accompany their masters to the imperial and local diets, where they exercised great influence by reason of their supe-

[1] Schmidt, *op. cit.*, pp. 16, 125. [2] Eichhorn, ii, § 269.
[3] The number of graduates of law at the University of Erfurt during the last half of the fifteenth century was triple that of the first half. In 1495 the University of Vienna was given the right to confer law degrees, and during the following five years it had three professors lecturing on Roman law. In 1456 the University of Greifswald had four teachers of the Code. In 1457 the University of Cologne was given the right to grant law degrees. The University of Heidelberg, founded in 1385, had up to 1444 only visiting lecturers on law; in 1469 it was given the right to confer degrees, and in 1498 a permanent professorship was founded and a full law faculty organized. In 1471 a complete law school was established in the city of Lüneburg by Emperor Frederick III. The University of Freiburg, founded in 1457, contained no provision for the study of law; but the demand for it was so great that in 1486 a regular teacher was appointed, and in 1490 a professorship was founded. At the foundation of the University of Basel in 1460 there were three law lecturers, and in 1495 a permanent faculty was organized. Stintzing, *Ulrich Zasius*, Beilage, ii; Stobbe, ii, pp. 20 *et seq.*

rior training and ability. The advent of the Roman lawyers as judges had begun with Emperor Charles IV, who appointed several to the higher imperial courts.¹ Their importance increased under Emperors Sigismund and Frederick III. They were often called upon to decide quarrels and claims between cities and princes.² By the end of the fifteenth century all the upper imperial and territorial courts were filled with men trained in the new system. In 1495 the highest imperial court, the *Reichskammergericht*, was declared the court of appeal for the whole German Empire, and was reorganized with the idea of making Roman law the basis of its procedure. One-half of its members had to be professional jurists and the other half, knights who had a knowledge of the principles of the Roman code.³ Roman jurists had dominated the upper courts of Bavaria since the middle of the fifteenth century, and those of Saxony since 1483. In 1495 half the judges of the upper courts in Würtemburg were required to be jurists, and they were soon in the majority. In 1503 the Elector Palatine Frederick I decreed that the members of the *Hofgerichte* or upper courts should all be jurists. The archbishop of Mainz issued a similar decree in 1516.⁴ The idea rapidly spread among the governing classes that only men learned in Roman law were fit to be judges. As the jurists increased in numbers and importance their dignity was correspondingly enhanced. They were put into the same rank as the lower nobility and were called *milites legum*.⁵

[1] Stobbe, i, p. 619.

[2] In 1424 a jurist decided a case between the archbishop of Magdeburg and the city of Halle. In 1429 another decided the ducal succession in Bavaria. Stobbe, i, p. 644.

[3] Stobbe, ii, p. 65.   [4] *Ibid.*, p. 92.   [5] *Ibid.*, i, p. 633.

The introduction into the town courts of this commanding code was even more quickly accomplished. The method generally followed was to appoint a jurist called a *Stadtschreiber* whose function it was to sit and advise with the judges. By the end of the fifteenth century nearly every city in Germany had such an officer. These men, merely advisors at first, because of their superior abilities powerfully influenced the procedure of the courts in the direction of Roman principles. Finally the *Stadtschreiber* absorbed the powers of the court and became the sole judge. If a city happened to contain a university, he was usually its professor of law. But he was so frequently called upon to advise cities and princes that he often neglected his professorial duties.[1] The most famous jurist of the day was Ulrich Zasius who was appointed in 1502 by the city of Freiburg to codify its laws and customs. He was also commissioned to draw up a model code for the margravate of Baden. Zasius was an acute legist of the most approved pattern. He utterly disregarded the local German laws and customs in his endeavor to apply the comprehensive principles of Roman jurisprudence to German conditions.[2]

Up to the beginning of the fifteenth century the lower courts which directly affected the mass of people were free from the presence of the Roman doctors. But not for long. The lower territorial courts very soon realized that they either had to adopt the new principles and methods or be reversed on appeal. Written proceedings were made mandatory in order to facilitate the regularly graded system of appeal contained in the Roman system. In spite of loud popular protest and opposition the ap-

[1] Stintzing, *Geschichte der deutschen Rechtswissenschaft*, p. 65.
[2] *Cf.* Stintzing, *Ulrich Zasius*, which gives a fine account of the work of this great jurist.

pointment of jurists to the lower courts became the order of the day.[1] The method of procedure according to German law, or rather local customs and traditions, largely unwritten, was in sharp contrast to that of the Roman. Every case tried under German law was brought before a sort of jury-court, called the *Schöffen*, composed of the free inhabitants of the district. This body tried the case and rendered the verdict which was pronounced by a presiding judge who was merely their mouthpiece. The part of the lawyer in these trials was insignificant. Sometimes the litigants would employ a mediator to speak for them, though generally they spoke for themselves. These courts were called together at irregular intervals and had to be re-formed anew every time they met. This lack of continuous organization produced uncertainty and had much to do with undermining their efficiency. Roman jurists were gradually introduced into these jury-courts in the following manner. The lord would appoint one as *Schultheiss*, who corresponded to the *Stadtschreiber* of the city. His original function was to sit with the *Schöffen* and advise with them. He soon made his influence felt, however, being generally much abler and more learned than his associates. He became the presiding officer and helped to formulate the judgment of the body, often imposing upon them his own opinions. Melanchthon complains that the jurists "lead the *Schöffen* around just as one leads a gentle cow by the nose." Finally the *Schultheiss* absorbed the authority of these jury-courts, which now in turn became merely advisory bodies.[2]

[1] Stobbe, ii, p. 83.
[2] Stölzel, *Die Entwicklung des gelehrten Richtertums in deutschen Territorien*, pp. 235 *et seq.*

Not only did the Roman jurist displace the German judges but his advent marked also the appearance in the German courts of the law for which he stood. He refused to recognize German law, declaring that a collection of local customs and traditions not having the will of a *princeps* as the source was not law at all. Hence he argued further that before the introduction of Roman law there was none. When cases came before them for trial they would always demand written evidence or authority and as German law was largely unwritten it was very easy to disregard it and substitute the Roman.[1] The jurist, now the sole arbiter, was appointed by the prince or lord, and his duty was to interpret a written code promulgated by the same authority. The machinery of justice being in complete control of the ruling powers, the subserviency of the jurists to the latter's interests was but natural. The lord could now easily work his will in the administration of justice since he both proclaimed the law and controlled the judge. Besides the *Schultheiss* there were two other territorial officers appointed by the lord: the *Amtmann*, a sort of sheriff or constable who looked after the peace of the district, and the *Rentmeister*, or steward, who kept a record of the dues and services owed by the peasants. Whatever independent power the village community had once enjoyed was now taken away and given over to a local bureaucracy in the pay of the lord and serving his interests.

Roman law was appropriate to an economic system based on a few great land-owners and a horde of slaves and dependents. Its ideal was that every individual was to seek his own advantage protected by the power of the state. The German law on the contrary was tinctured

---

[1] Stobbe, ii, pp. 119 *et seq.*

with communal ethics and emphasized the welfare of the group as against that of the individual. The holding of common lands, so fully recognized by German customs, was an example of their spirit of neighborliness. The new jurisprudence had the effect of undermining the personal status of the German peasant. Roman law did not recognize the various gradations of personally free peasants varying from those with very few dues and services to others with very many, the amount, however, in most cases being definite and limited. It included only gradations of the personally unfree,—the *colonus* or serf and the *servus* or slave. The tendency, already strong, to reduce a comparatively free and prosperous peasantry to a state of hopeless serfdom by increasing dues and services, confiscating common lands and enforcing severe game laws, received a fresh impetus through the introduction of this ancient ideal. The jurists were of great service to the lords in getting up legal quibbles to despoil the peasant of his rights. They declared German leases to be limited, and many peasants were ousted from their life-holdings because they could show no documentary proof of ownership. The free German peasant found himself sliding very rapidly into the position of a Roman *colonus*.[1] A popular skit by the satirist Thomas Mürner runs thus:

> "Es ist ein Volk, das seyndt Juristen
> Wie seyndt mir das so sölliche Christen
> Sie thunt das Recht so spitzig bügen
> Und könnens wo man will hinfügen
> Darnach wirt Recht fälschlich Ohnrecht
> Das macht manchen armen knecht!"[2]

The legal tyranny of the lord could be more easily ex-

[1] Janssen, i, pp. 570-576.
[2] Quoted by Zimmerman, i, p. 126.

ercised now that he was *dominus* under Roman law. Free peasants were arbitrarily put into prison or whipped. The communities of Oepfingen and Griesingen complain that "when a peasant appealed for justice, the lord seized him by the throat and said 'I'll give you justice,' and straightway put him into prison."[1] The question whether a peasant could sue a lord came up before the Diet of Freiburg in 1498 but was referred to the Diet of Augsburg in 1500 which decided that he could sue, but not the lord whose subject he was.[2] This decree was useless to the peasant as there was little likelihood of his suing any other lord than his own. True, he had the right to appeal to higher courts; but this too was practically useless as the lord of the manor was often the political lord of the district and so controlled the higher as well as the lower courts. Hence in the long run, the peasant was still subject to the legal will of his lord. Sometimes the former had to promise before the trial took place not to appeal. The peasants of Rottenacker complain that "when two peasants come to trial they must give the lord a written promise not to appeal from the decision of his court."[3] There was a complete loss of confidence in the fairness and justice of the judiciary and a common proverb was,

"Das edle Recht ist worden krank
Den Armen kurz, den Reichen lang."

The hatred of Roman jurists prevailed among all classes of society because of numerous long-drawn-out trials which were both expensive and uncertain. They were denounced as law-twisters, heathen, thieves and

[1] Vogt, *Die Corresp. des s. B. Ulrich Arzt*, nos. 889 and 893.
[2] Zimmerman, i, p. 127.   [3] *Ibid.*, no. 896.

blood-suckers in the pamphlet literature of the day. *Ein jurist ein böser Christ* became a common saying. The satirist Sebastian Brant in a doggerel entitled "*Knight and Jurist*" says: "The robber-knight steals openly, the lawyer, secretly. The former exposes his body to danger and storm, the latter sneaks behind his inkstand. The one burns and destroys, the other roasts the peasant with papers."[1] Johann Cochläus, a champion of the Church, asked "Why so many suits over trifles if not to fill the pockets of the lawyers? How quickly all would be settled were it not for their subtleties! I blame no one personally, I only lament the general evil which has come from that Thracian fellow, Justinian."[2] Like the bureaucracy of the princes, the jurists were very fertile in inventing new taxes. "This doctor is not yet learned in the law," sarcastically remarked the theologian Trithemius, "because he has not invented a new tax."[3] To the popular mind the jurist appeared as the enemy of the people, who was ever ready to serve the governing and exploiting classes. "Their influence is very evil," declares Wimpheling, "because for the sake of money they promote the interests of the great companies and other vampires of the people. They become the favorites of the great princes by showing them how to destroy the rights and liberties of the estates. As judges and secret councilors they confuse and destroy what the wisdom of our ancestors have built up."[4] Ulrich von Hutten, the spokesman of the knights, whose independent existence was threatened by the rising power of the princes, was especially bitter against the jurists. "Above all things," he says, "they

---

[1] Brant, *Narrenschiff*, no. 79.
[2] Janssen, i, p. 566.
[3] *Ibid.*, p. 571.
[4] *Ibid.*, p. 569.

take an odious pride in their subtlety in transforming everything, particularly the government. Of what sort of stuff are these lawyers made? If the princes only knew how light are these fellows who appear so weighty! ...... Honest men are circumvented by their trickery and the laws they twist as it pleases them. Hence justice is corrupted."[1]

At the beginning of the sixteenth century Germany was flooded with these Roman lawyers, many of whom were *Halbgelehrten* or "shysters," whose trickery, dishonesty and subserviency became proverbial. Wimpheling, writing in 1507, complains that there is "a horde of rascals who regard law only as a means to fill their pockets, who manufacture law suits in order to bleed the common man."[2] The great jurist, Zasius, was moved to thunder against these disreputables. "They show merely shallow learning," he declared, "not real knowledge. ...... Their trickery poisons the courts, makes the judges ridiculous, disturbs the peace and confuses the administration. Such people are hated by God and man."[3] Bitterness of feeling against the Roman doctors was so rife that no plan of reform was considered complete without an article aimed against their influence.[4] The lawyer had become the common scapegoat whose destruction all classes united in demanding. "Who would not rejoice," exclaims Wimpheling, "if the knights, burghers and peasants, loyal to the old customs, were to unite themselves and war manfully against

[1] Böcking's edition, iv, p. 381.
[2] Janssen, i, p. 566.
[3] Stintzing, *Geschichte, etc.*, p. 161.
[4] It became a common custom, when making agreements or contracts, to insert a provision that no jurist was to be employed in case of error or dispute. Eichhorn, iii, p. 344.

these enemies, whose deceit and sophistry has done so much to undermine them? It would be a struggle vital to the people's interest."[1] These protests resulted in some measures, particularly in Bavaria and Würtemburg. In 1463 Duke Johann of Bavaria was forced to promise that he would not appoint jurists to his courts and would eradicate all Roman law.[2] In 1471 the Landtag of Bavarian Estates at Landshut complained that "the offices are filled with strangers, who continually introduce new methods, which is greatly against our freedom."[3] In 1497 the Estates declared that "the doctors in the courts are so numerous that they have more influence than the German judges, and they do not render proper and fair judgements."[4] In 1506 they demanded that "the courts shall be officered with honorable German judges."[5] In 1514 the Estates of Würtemburg again complained to the duke that "since the doctors have come, there has been an increase of all kinds of dues and services. The judges in the courts should be German, not Roman doctors. The jurists should be dismissed because now it costs ten gulden to try a case, whereas twelve years ago, before they came, it cost only ten shillings. The doctors are now to be found in the villages, where they are active in inventing new dues to be squeezed from the people. Such activity is harmful and should be stopped."[6]

In spite of denunciation, protests of diets, promises by princes, the jurists continued to find lucrative employ-

[1] Janssen, i, p. 569.
[2] Franklin, *Beiträge zur Geschichte der Reception des röm. Rechts in Deut.*, i, p. 20.
[3] *Ibid.*, p. 22.   [4] *Ibid.*, p. 24.
[5] *Ibid.*, p. 30.   [6] Stobbe, ii, p. 51.

ment. Their services were too valuable to those in power to cause a really serious effort to be made to oust them. Roman law continued to develop in Germany undisturbed, and by the end of the sixteenth century the old German law had practically disappeared. It had been either discarded or absorbed by the foreign code.

CHAPTER III

THE PEASANTS' REVOLT

IT is doubtful whether the peasant in the time of Luther was in any worse condition than his ancestors in the fourteenth century. Many instances are cited by the Catholic historian Janssen of the prosperity of the German peasant in the fifteenth and early sixteenth centuries. He writes of Carinthian farmers who wore finer clothes and drank better wine than nobles, and of those in Altenburg who wore caps and coats of fine bear pelt.[1] Jacob Wimpheling, the humanist, writes of the extraordinary well-being of the Alsatian peasants. "Their prosperity here," he says, "and in most parts of Germany has made them proud and luxurious. I know peasants who spend as much at the marriage of their sons and daughters or the baptism of their children as would buy a small house and farm or vineyard. They are extravagant in their dress and living, and drink costly wines."[2]

Notwithstanding these evidences of prosperity, the condition of the peasantry was rapidly deteriorating. At the beginning of the sixteenth century very few in-

---

[1] Janssen, i, pp. 366-371. It should be borne in mind that it is the purpose of Janssen to disprove the statements of Protestant historians that Germany was in a bad plight before Luther's advent. Hence he is very assiduous in giving every proof of Germany's prosperity at the opening of the 16th century.

[2] *Ibid.*, i, p. 369.

deed were independent proprietors of the land they cultivated, with representation in the local diets, which in the Middle Ages was a sign of class independence and equality. These conditions existed only in the Tyrol and Friesland. The vast majority were *Hörige*, a class personally free but whose land was subject to dues, the individuals being liable to services according to agreement, *Pachtzins*. This agreement might be perpetual, *Erbpacht*, or for a definite period of time, *Zeitpacht*. Their lord might be a prince, count, knight, bishop, abbot or city. Within this class of *Hörige* there was great variation; from the type that merely paid yearly ground rent to those who were so overloaded with dues and services that their condition bordered on serfdom. The lowest class of peasants were the unfree, the serfs or *Leibeigene*, whose condition differed from the *Hörige*, not necessarily in the amount of dues and services, but in the fact that these were unlimited and indefinite. The lord could demand from the *Leibeigener* all his labor and everything he produced, though in many places local customs imposed certain limitations. Compared to the number of *Hörige*, the unfree peasants were very few and they lived mainly in Pomerania.[1]

It was the *Hörige* who were the backbone of all the agrarian uprisings. This middle-class peasant, living in a semi-independent community near the estate of the lord, became aware that the increase of dues and services was transforming him into a state of practical serfdom, and the village common into a part of the lord's manor. There were two kinds of dues, produce or money, and *Fronen* or bodily services. The peasant had to give to

[1] See Grimm, *Weisthümer*, ii, for full and detailed descriptions of the classes, dues and services of peasants.

his lord a definite percentage twice a year, at spring and harvest, of all his field, garden, forest and animal products. Besides, there were special demands at feasts, births, baptisms, marriages and deaths. The lord demanded Easter chickens, Christmas chickens, Shrovetide hens, etc. There was a constant succession of dues, taxes and services, squeezed from the peasant on every pretext.[1] Should a storm, frost or flood injure the crop, it made no difference in the collection of the amount due. The peasants of Fürstenberg complain that "it often happens when hail or wind does harm to our crops or when there is a bad season, our lords refuse to reduce their demands and require as much as in a good year."[2] The peasants of Brunnen declare that "when fire, flood or hail afflicts us, the lord as well as we should suffer."[3]

Most irksome of all were the *Fronen* or unrewarded services in the chase, fishing and labor on the personal estate of the lord. The peasant had to drop work on his own farm, no matter how urgent, in order to perform these services. The number of days required varied with the locality. In the duchy of Austria it was twelve days a year; in other parts of Germany the peasant had to work for the lord all of April and May. Generally the number of *Fronen* days varied with the occupations on the farm, as one day's haying, one day's harvesting, corning, etc.[4] The peasants of Stühlingen complain:

One day we must cut wheat, another day bind, on others plow, sow, thresh, cut hay and cart it to the barn, make fences

[1] Grimm, *Rechtsalterthümer*, pp. 358-394.
[2] Baumann, *Akten zur Geschichte, etc.*, p. 211.
[3] *Die Corresp. d. s. B. Ulrich Arzt*, no. 889.
[4] Grimm, *Rechtsalterthümer*, p. 355.

and help in the chase. We must provide wood, not only for fire but for building, and pile it in heaps. Often when we can least spare the time, we must dig roots and pick berries for the lord. Our wives or helpers must also prepare the flax till it is ready for spinning. We are forced to drain the creeks, which, as we need the water, does us harm. We must cart his corn, mow, and clean the stables three times a year. We must take care of the cattle of the castle-warden also and then help in the hunt.[1]

While at work for the lord the peasant received free food and lodging. Janssen gives many instances of their good treatment; of the red wine, two kinds of meat, soups and barley-bread, that the lords gave the *Fröner* who at times was even royally entertained with music and dancing.[2] Doubtless all this was true in some places, though it did not have the effect of reconciling the worker to his unrewarded tasks. In an anonymous pamphlet quoted by Zimmerman, the writer exclaims: "In what code has God given you the right to demand of us poor peasants services on your fields and compel us to neglect our own crops over which we labor in sweat and blood? In addition we poor people must give you all sorts of dues and taxes. Hence we, our wives and children have not enough of bread, salt and bacon."[3]

The church, too, took her share of the peasant's harvest. There were three tithes, each about 10 per cent, payable yearly; one called the "great tithe" on corn, rye, oats, wheat and wine; another called the "small tithe" on fruit and vegetables; and a third called the "flesh tithe" on domestic animals.

Every event in the life of the peasant was made the

[1] Baumann, *Akten*, p. 199.   [2] Janssen, i, p. 333.
[3] Zimmerman, i, p. 131.

occasion for new dues; and the more grevious the event the heavier were the dues. Nearly every peasant manifesto complains bitterly of the *Todfall* or heriot.¹ According to universal custom in case of the death of the head of the family, the lord had the right to take from the widow the most valuable article (*Besthaupt*) her husband had left—the best cow, horse or even dress.² Often it was commuted for a money payment and ultimately became a regular death tax.³ In case the dead peasant was a *Leibeigener* the *Todfall* was everything he had. "When a man or woman dies," complain the peasants of the monastery of Kempten, "an emissary from the monastery comes and takes an inventory of all the goods. No matter how many children the dead person leaves behind him, whether he was rich or poor, one half of the estate is always taken. When an unmarried peasant dies, all his property is seized by the abbot and nothing is given to father, mother, brother or sister."⁴ The amount paid in heriot, whether in money or in kind, differed with the customs of the locality. In Lower Austria it was 5 per cent of the estate, in Upper Austria it was 10 per cent, in Carinthia 14⅔ per cent and in Würtemburg from 10 to 15 per cent.⁵ The smaller the estate, the harder it was for the survivors to bear even the loss of a little, as death had already taken away the bread-winner from the family. The peasants of Attenweiler complain that, "when one dies, then comes the lord and shares

---

¹ See Art. XI of the Twelve Articles, *cf. infra*, p. 145. Also Baumann, *Akten*, p. 190. The articles of the peasants of Odenwald and Neckarthal demand that "the *Todfall* shall be abolished and never again collected." Oechsle, p. 290.
² Grimm, *Weisthümer*, ii, p. 526.
³ *Ibid.*, i, p. 284.   ⁴ Baumann, *Akten*, p. 51.
⁵ Vogt, *Die Vorgeschichte des Bauernkriegs*, p. 10.

the estate with the wife. We think it wrong that he should have the right to inherit of us."[1]

The lower aristocracy had also been profoundly affected by the political and economic changes in the sixteenth century. The growing importance of trade caused a shifting of values from land to commerce. The knight found himself growing impoverished and isolated. The continuous division of estates through the sharing of inheritance by all the children, had reduced the size of his holdings. Gunpowder had deprived him of military importance and the rapid growth of the power of the great princes was undermining his independent political position. The magnificence and luxury of the great merchants of the cities excited his envy and his emulation. The demands of his position could be satisfied only in one way; namely by getting more and more out of the peasants. The latter everywhere bitterly complained of continual increases in dues and services. When the peasant rose in the morning he never could tell what new dues and services awaited him. "In our times," say the peasants of the monastery of Kempten, "the dues on our property increase more and more. It was not so in the days of our forefathers, whose needs were less than ours."[2] The services too, were continually changed. Old ones were increased and new ones added. The peasants of Rottenacker declare:

> Formerly if we paid thirty shillings, we were released from hay service; but now we pay the money and are compelled to do the work besides. . . . The custom was that we had to pay one gulden instead of the war service of ten men . . . but our lord demanded three gulden. We argued, begging him

[1] *Die Corresp. des s. B. Ulrich Arzt*, no. 881.
[2] *Ibid.*, pp. 64, 70.

to relent, and instead he now asks five gulden. For such reasons the community becomes poor. When we finally paid him the five gulden, he cursed us as faithless rascals. This was undeserved, for we were perfectly willing to do what was reasonable.[1]

"Every year," declare the peasants of Göschweiler, "we used to plow for our lord no more than an acre and a quarter and it was considered sufficient; but now he compells us to plow more and in addition to thresh wheat and oats and cart hay."[2]

There was thus a well-defined tendency for the free peasant to fall into a condition of helplessness, subject to arbitrary and indefinite demands. He was becoming merely the occupier of a transferable and alienable piece of land, in short, a kind of *colonus*, like that of ancient Rome, or perhaps even a *servus*. It was a common saying that the *Freier* was becoming a *Höriger* and the *Höriger* a *Leibeigener*.

Perhaps the most insidious attack upon peasant independence was the overreaching desire on the part of the lords to seize the common lands. Each village community had a common district or mark, called *allgemeine*, *allmeine* or *almende*, which consisted of forest, meadow and heath. Every permanent free inhabitant of the village had the right to pasture his animals there and gather wood from the forest. In the middle of the fifteenth century the lords began persistently to encroach upon the common lands by setting up regulations limiting their use by the peasants, by reviving old feudal rights or by simply using force. In 1502 the peasants living under the lordship of the abbot of Och-

[1] *Die Corresp. des s. B. Ulrich Arzt*, no. 896.
[2] Baumann, *Akten*, p. 225.

senhausen in upper Swabia declared that '"the prelate has made smaller our common lands by adding parts to the property of the monastery ...... This took place in spite of the protests of the community."[1] The peasants of Rottenacker declare that "formerly our lord had the right to pasture three or four head of cattle in our meadows, now he sends twenty or thirty. Hence some villages have to be turned into pasture lands."[2] "From of old we have been entitled to the use of the common forest, meadow and stream," complain the peasants of Fürstenberg, "but our lords have taken them away from us by force and without any show of right."[3]

The process of taking over the common lands assumed an appearance of righteous legality when the lord happened to be a territorial prince, as he could then set up a claim of overlordship. The introduction of Roman law did much to hasten the process. When a dispute over the use of forest, meadow or stream between the peasants and their lord came before the Roman jurist, the decision was invariably given in favor of the lord, as Roman law recognized the principle of private property exclusively. The idea of communal holding, so ingrained in the life of the German peasantry during the Middle Ages, was entirely foreign, both in spirit and in letter, to the Roman law. Frederick the Victorious, Elector Palatine, got a decision from a Roman jurist giving him supreme right over all common lands in his territory.[4] Severe laws were passed against the use of forests,

---

[1] Egelhaaf, *Analekten zur Geschichte des Bauernkriegs*, p. 544.
[2] *Die Corresp. des s. B. Ulrich Arzt*, no. 896.
[3] Baumann, *Akten*, p. 209.
[4] Bezold, *Geschichte der deutschen Reformation*, p. 45; Mone in *Zeitschrift für die Geschichte des Oberrheins*, i, p. 393.

meadows and streams by anybody except the lord of the district. The resentment of the peasants on this score was particularly bitter, and three of the Twelve Articles deal with the subject.[1] By the time of the Protestant Revolution the control of the common lands had slipped into the hands of the lords, and the once independent village community became part of the manorial estate. The aristocratic sport of hunting, always so fruitful in arousing the anger of the husbandman in all ages, was another source of exasperation to the German farmer. The killing of crop-destroying game by peasants was forbidden under severe penalties. In 1517 the Duke of Würtemburg decreed that any peasant found off the marked paths in the woods and fields of the game preserves, carrying a gun, cross-bow or any other fire arm shall lose both his eyes.[2] The peasants of Stühlingen complain that "those animals which do us harm, we are forbidden to hunt, kill or scare away; and to disobey is to have one's eyes put out. It is only right and fair that we should be allowed to shoot these animals."[3] The peasants were often called upon to assist in the destruction of their own crops by beating the bushes, running after the hounds and furnishing horses and wagons to the huntsmen. The Kisslegger tenants complain that "we have to run after the game all day without food and drink and at times we are so tired that we can hardly walk, and we receive our pay in curses and kicks."[4]

[1] Articles IV, V, X. [2] Bezold, p. 45.
[3] Baumann, *Akten*, p. 212. This community also complained of the destruction of crops by the hunters. "As we must with great care and cost till our ground in order to support our wives and children, therefore our lords and their servants ought to be careful not to do us harm; but they ride and run over our fields in their hunts just at the time when most harm can be done to our crops." (p. 194).
[4] *Ibid.*, no. 167.

Loaded with dues and getting smaller returns because of the fall of land values, the peasant was forced to have recourse to the capitalist of the city. In order to raise money he was often obliged to mortgage his farm at usurious rates of interest.[1] The capitalist who held the mortgage on the land of a free peasant was not satisfied with collecting the interest but demanded dues besides as though he were the lord.[2] "This may be called usury or not," says Martin Luther, "but it does the same work, as lands, cities, lords and people are burdened, fleeced and ruined."[3] A popular cartoon of the day represents a peasant, with a sack on his shoulder, standing cap in hand before a money-lender, who sits complacently behind a table heaped with gold coins. Foreclosure of mortgages became so common that, as Luther said, "anyone who had a hundred gulden to invest could gobble up a peasant a year with no more danger to his life and property than there is in sitting near a stove and roasting apples."[4] Often the crop was sold or mortgaged before it was even grown, and the merchant who advanced the money could easily make his own terms with the needy farmer. The outcry against this sort of thing was so great that the Diet of Nuremberg in 1522 decreed that no merchant should be allowed to advance money to peasants on the security of their growing crops, since the interest he gets he does not earn.[5] The condition of the peasant had so degenerated that a common saying was,

[1] It was quite common for the peasant to pay from thirty to eighty per cent. See Lamprecht, *Zum Verständniss, etc.*, p. 234.
[2] Bensen, *Geschichte des Bauernkriegs in Ostfranken*, p. 25.
[3] *Werke* (Erlangen), xx, p. 110.
[4] Bezold, p. 452.
[5] *Deutsche Reichstagsakten*, iii, p. 592.

Der Bauer ist an Ochsen statt,
Nur dass er keine Hörner hat.

The harder became his lot the more was the peasant idealized. He was often extolled in the popular literature of the day as the honest toiler, on whose labor all the other classes depended; as the examplar of homely, honest, simple Christian virtues, God's truest nobleman. The halo of "honest toil" that never fails to encircle the head of the down-trodden was already his.[1]

The collection of the dues and services by the lord was exploitation, pure and simple, as he contributed nothing towards its production either as manager or capitalist. He simply took what the peasant produced, in order to be able to fight, feast and play. The protection that the lord formerly gave him in return for all this was no longer needed in the sixteenth century when strong governments had been established throughout the empire. The German peasant of 1525, like the French peasant of 1789, "no longer looked up to his lord as his ruler and protector, but viewed him as a sort of legalized robber who demanded a share of his precious harvest, whose officers awaited the farmer at the crossing of the river to claim a toll, who would not let him sell his produce when he wished, or permit him to protect his fields from the ravages of the pigeons which it pleased the lord to keep."[2]

The first peasant uprising since the great Hussite movement in Bohemia took place in the southern part of Germany in 1476. Like all other revolts in the Middle Ages, it had a religious coloring. A peasant-piper

---

[1] Bezold, *Die armen Leute, etc.*, pp. 32 et seq.

[2] J. H. Robinson, *An Introduction to the History of Western Europe*, p. 545.

named Hans Böheim, living in Niklashausen, near the city of Würzburg, declared one day that a revelation had come to him from the Virgin, that henceforth there was to be no authority, lay or spiritual; taxes were to be abolished and all earthly goods were to be held in common. Niklashausen soon became a sort of shrine and Hans a prophet to thousands who came to hear him preach. It was not long before an active rebellion was on foot. An army of 34,000 peasants assembled one Sunday at the command of the preacher. The bishop of Würzburg, the feudal lord of the district, becoming aware of the rebellious character of the assembly, caused Hans to be kidnaped. He then scattered the peasants with great slaughter.[1]

In 1491 occurred the rebellion of the peasants of the monastery of Kempten in Bavaria. The abbot, who was the lord of a vast territory, had tried by means of forged documents to reduce the peasants to serfdom and to confiscate the common lands. Like the former, this uprising was also unsuccessful.[2]

In 1493 the Alsatian peasants of the Bishop of Strassburg organized a secret movement to abolish all debts, tithes, dues, etc. They took as their emblem a laced shoe of the kind usually worn by peasants, called a *Bundschuh*, a representation of which was emblazoned on the banners carried by them. The *Bundschuh* from now on became the symbol of peasant uprisings. This rebellion in Alsatia was put down with much bloodshed.[3]

[1] K. M. Barack, "Hans Böheim und die Wallfahrt nach Niklashausen im Jahre 1476" in *Archiv des hist. Vereins von Unterf. und Aschaffenburg*, vol. xiv, pp. 1-108.

[2] Zimmerman, *Allgemeine Geschichte des grossen Bauernkriegs*, i, chap. i.

[3] Zimmerman, i, pp. 141-145.

In 1502 another *Bundschuh* took place in the bishopric of Speyer. A league numbering 7000 men and 400 women bound themselves by oath to take away the property of the nobles and clergy and to abolish all dues and services. In order to be free they declared, "we will fight with arms and swords because we mean to be like the Swiss." After a bloody struggle, the uprising was quelled.[1]

In 1512 occurred the most threatening of all the *Bundschuhs*. Joss Fritz, a survivor of the last uprising, organized another at Lehen in Baden. His purpose was to abolish all authority except that of the pope and emperor. All feudal burdens were to be done away with; the property of the monasteries was to be confiscated and distributed among the poor. Fishing, hunting and pasturing were to be free to all. The revolt was rapidly organized through a system of secret groups or "circles." The movement however was betrayed and put down by the authorities.[2]

In 1514 there arose in the dukedom of Würtemburg a concerted movement of the peasants under the leadership of a picturesque character named "Poor Conrad." It was largely due to the tyranny of the Duke Ulrich, whose extravagance had overburdened the people with taxes. In this uprising the peasants were joined by many of the townspeople; but it, too, failed like the others and was suppressed with great cruelty.[3]

The great Peasants' Revolt of 1525 was the culmination of these agrarian disturbances. For a century after

---

[1] R. Herold, *Der Bundschuh im Bistum Speyer von Jahre 1502*.

[2] H. Schreiber, *Der Bundschuh zu Lehen und der arme Konrad*.

[3] For further description of the peasant movements before the great revolt of 1525 see R. Zöllner, *Zur Vorgeschichte des Bauernkriegs*, and C. Ullmann, *Reformatoren vor der Reformation*.

the Hussite movement, discontent had been rife among the peasantry of Germany, yet the revolts were sporadic and confined mainly to definite localities. It needed the unifying element of religious revolt furnished by Luther to bring about a general uprising throughout the German Empire. From the little village of Stühlingen, in the Black Forest, came the signal for the great uprising that very quickly spread all over Germany. According to tradition, the wife of the lord of the village, Count Lupfen, demanded of her tenants that they gather strawberries and snail-shells for her. This slight impost provoked vigorous resistance. A leader appeared among the peasants named Hans Müller of Bulgenbach, who quickly gathered around him 1200 men and marched to the forest town of Waldshut. As he marched through the country-side he left behind him a network of peasant organizations called Evangelical Brotherhoods. The authorities, becoming alarmed, summoned the Swabian League, a voluntary association of princes and cities claiming to act as the representative of the emperor in preserving public order.

About the same time the peasants of Upper Swabia began to stir. The center of discontent was in the territory of the Abbot of Kempten, whose oppression and cruelty had won him the bitter hatred of his tenants. An assembly of his peasants took place which presented a list of grievances to their lord, the abbot. But he refused to pay the slightest attention to their complaints.[1] Accordingly three contingents of peasants from Baltringen, the Black Forest and Lake Constance held a conference in the city of Memmingen, where they organized

[1] Baumann, *Akten*, pp. 378-387.

themselves into a Christian Brotherhood and adopted the famous Twelve Articles.[1]

Meanwhile, George Truchsess, the commander-in-chief of the forces of the Swabian League, mustered 8000 foot and 3000 horse of *Landesknechte* or German condottieri. He attacked and captured the town of Leipheim, defended by the peasants under Jacob Wehe, their pastor, who was tried on the charge of being a rebel and executed.[2] The peasants were not disheartened by this reverse, and their movement continued to spread rapidly. Bands of armed men roamed the country, burning and plundering castles and monasteries and demanding allegiance to the Twelve Articles. Many knights, out of fear, were forced to take service with them and became their leaders.

At no time during the revolt was there anything resembling a continued campaign, but instead, a series of spontaneous attacks and independent negotiations by various bands. A body of 2000 peasants called the United Contingent, under the command of two ex-innkeepers, Jäcklein Rohrbach and George Metzler, captured the castle of the Count of Hohenlohe, situated near the imperial city of Heilbronn, and compelled the the count to accept the Twelve Articles and become a member of the Evangelical Brotherhood.[3]

At Weinsberg, a town near Heilbronn, the peasants were guilty of an outrage which greatly aroused public opinion against them and their cause. Count von Helfenstein, the lord of the district, had made himself particularly obnoxious by massacring a body of peasants

---

[1] *Cf. infra*, pp. 132 *et seq.*
[2] Baumann, *Akten*, pp. 181–184.
[3] Zimmerman, ii, pp. 271–277.

without warning. His tenants, eager for revenge, under the leadership of Jäcklein Rohrbach, who had a private grudge to satisfy, stormed the castle. The count and many of his knights were taken and put to death with revolting cruelty. His wife, who was a natural daughter of the emperor, was insulted and driven around in a dung-cart. The massacre of Weinsberg aroused a storm of indignation throughout Germany.[1] A peasant band under Wendel Hipler and George Metzler captured Heilbronn and forced the city to contribute men and money to their cause. Only the houses of the Teutonic knights, who were particularly hated by the common man, were plundered.

Among those who were attracted to the standard of the rebels were many impoverished knights, who, while not sympathizing with the aims of the common people saw a chance for booty and adventure. Particularly were they anxious to satisfy their grudge against the the great princes, who a short time before, had put down their insurrection under Franz von Sickingen. Hence they shared with the peasants in the common hatred of the great lords. Such a knight was the famous Götz von Berlichingen, the hero of Goethe's drama.[2] He had at first offered his services to the Swabian League, but for some reason or other they were refused; so he became the commander-in-chief of the peasant forces. His appointment meant the domination of the more conservative element represented by Hipler and Weigand whose plan of reform was even more conservative than the Twelve Articles.[3] Their great object was to form a working alliance between the peasants and the knights

[1] Bax, *Peasants' War*, pp. 126 *et seq.;* Janssen, ii, pp. 535-537.
[2] See Götz's *Lebensbeschreibung.* [3] *Cf. infra*, pp. 126 *et seq.*

on the basis of a common hostility to the great princes and prelates. The United Contingent now under the command of Götz von Berlichingen marched to Mainz and compelled the prince-archbishop to pay a ransom of 15,000 gulden. In the cities, meanwhile, an internal struggle was going on. Encouraged by the success of the common man in the country, the town proletariat began to rise and demand a share in the government. Often there was coöperation between the peasants outside and the lower classes inside the cities. In Rothenburg-on-the-Tauber, the populace rose under the leadership of a blind monk named Hans Schmidt. The houses of the Teutonic knights were attacked and plundered. The ruling patriciate was ousted from power and the city government re-organized on a communistic basis.[1] "There is great division in the towns," wrote the Bavarian Chancellor Eck, "those among the Lutherans that are poor take the side of the peasants; the non-Catholics and the wealthy Lutherans are opposed to the peasants."[2]

The leader of the Franconian peasants was the gallant knight Florian Geyer. Unlike Götz, he willingly and sincerely espoused the peasant cause. During the entire revolt, his loyalty, devotion and bravery were never questioned. At the head of his famous regiment, the Black Troop, a well-disciplined body of veteran soldiers, he moved on the city of Würzburg. On the way, there was the usual burning and plundering of monasteries and castles. "They fell on the monasteries," writes Lorenz Fries the bishop's secretary, "on the chests and

[1] Bax, pp. 154 *et seq.*
[2] Vogt, "Die bayerische Politik," p. 402.

the cellars of the priests and gluttonously consumed whatever they found. It pleased the 'Brotherhood' exceedingly that they could eat and drink without paying. More drunken, more gluttonous and more helpless folk were not seen during the rebellion. I know not whether from their conduct, apart from fire and bloodshed, this peasant war ought not to be called a wine war."[1] Florian Geyer found the city of Würzburg in a state of insurrection against its lord, the bishop. The gates were opened; he marched in at the head of his troop and received an enthusiastic welcome from the citizens.

The visionary element in the revolt found its classic expression in Thomas Münzer, a type of wandering preacher and pamphleteer, to whom Lutheranism was but a gateway to far more radical ideas of religion. Fundamentally, Münzer was a theologian who became interested in politics, by the new turn of affairs in the religious agitation. His power over the peasants was largely due to fervid oratory, of which he was a past master. He came to Alstätt in Thuringia, where he very soon was at the head of a sect of visionaries, who preached the millenium and the second coming of Christ. Münzer at first appealed to the rulers to champion his ideas but failing to get their support, he turned to the common people. His ideas of how the world was to be changed were typical of the religious mystic, turned social reformer. Society was to be reorganized on a communistic basis, and the primitive church was taken as a model. There were to be no rulers and no subjects; neither rich nor poor. From Alstätt poured a stream of pamphlets, written by Münzer, denouncing the wealthy and powerful and demanding the death of all who refused

[1] Bax, p. 164.

to accept his "Gospel." Luther he scorned as the "soft-living flesh of Wittenberg," the tool of the lords and princes. At the instance of Luther, Münzer was driven out of Alstätt by the authorities. He fled to Mühlhausen where, by joining with Heinrich Pfeiffer, an ex-friar and leader of the town proletariat, he succeeded in expelling the governing patriciate. Backed by the lower classes, they got control of the town council, and what had taken place in Alstätt was now repeated in Mühlhausen.

The sensational doings of Münzer in Thuringia have caused many historians to exaggerate his importance in the Peasants' Revolt. In truth, his activities were rather a digression from its fundamental objects. Münzer took up the peasants' cause with the idea of bettering, not their condition, but their souls. At bottom he was the *reductio ad absurdum* of a Luther. The Twelve Articles, not the fantastic notions of this confused prophet, were the legitimate expressions of the ideals of the peasants.[1]

All this while the governing classes were paralyzed by fear and inaction. The successes of the peasants at last roused them to a sense of their danger. The forces of the Swabian League under George Truchsess, strengthened by additional men and supplies, began an active campaign. They met an army of peasants massed at Frankenhausen in Thuringia. There, on March 15, 1525, the rebels sustained a fearful rout and were compelled to flee in great disorder. More than 5000 of them were slain in a few hours. Münzer escaped, but was captured and executed.[2] The defeat of Frankenhausen broke the back of the rebellion and proved the turning-point of the

---

[1] For further details of Münzer see J. K. Seidemann, *Thomas Münzer, eine Biographie;* O. Merx, *Thomas Münzer und Heinrich Pfeiffer, 1523–1525.*

[2] For further details see Bax, pp. 262 *et seq.*

war. The suppression of the revolt was now a matter of days. Truchsess defeated an army of 12,000 men in Würtemburg and laid waste many villages. He then attacked the city of Heilbronn, defended by Hipler; the city was taken and Hipler's force dispersed. To recapture Würzburg was the object of the next move. On the way thither, the Black Troop of Florian Geyer was surprised and cut to pieces. Würzburg was easily regained and this practically ended all organized resistence.

The chief reason for the rapid collapse of the peasants' movement was the lack of common direction. They had not learned to unite into large bodies and plan anything resembling a campaign. The result was that the trained forces of the Swabian League had no difficulty in defeating the various ill-armed and undisciplined bands.

The suppression of the revolt was unparalleled in cruelty and blood-shed. It is reckoned that over 100,000 peasants lost their lives. Fields, houses and barns were pillaged and destroyed by the ruthless lords. Thousands were ruined and thousands more became homeless fugitives.[1] The authorities were determined to take full revenge for the outrages committed by the peasants at the beginning of the revolt. Services and dues became more onerous than ever before and the German peasantry sank into a condition of hopeless despair. A contemporary pamphlet says: "Houses are burned; fields and vineyards lie fallow; clothes and household goods are stolen or burned; cattle and sheep are taken away; and likewise horses and trappings. The prince, the gentleman or the nobleman will have his rent and due. Eternal God! whither shall the widows and the poor children go forth to seek it."[2]

---

[1] Köstlin, i, pp. 714 *et seq.*   [2] Bax, p. 356.

CHAPTER IV

THE ATTITUDE OF MARTIN LUTHER TOWARD THE PEASANTS' REVOLT

THE attitude of Martin Luther toward the Peasants' Revolt has been a subject of acrimonious dispute among Catholics, Protestants and Socialists. The Catholic historian Janssen denounces Luther as being at first partly responsible for the movement and then deserting it when the interests of his patrons, the princes, were threatened.[1] Protestant apologists, on the other hand, his biographer Köstlin for instance, defend Luther, urging that he took a rational course in emphasizing the principles of the Reformation against revolutionary visionaries who would have brought about anarchy and ruin.[2] Others, like the modern Socialist, Belfort Bax, denounce him as a tool of the princes and a traitor to the peasants' cause.[3] Luther's attitude will be best understood after an inquiry into his general views of society, government and reform.

In a widely circulated pamphlet entitled *On Secular Authority and How Far it Should be Obeyed*, issued in 1523, Luther indulged in severe denunciation of princes in general. "One should know," he declares,

that from the beginning of the world a clever prince has been a

---
[1] Janssen, ii, pp. 372-418; 519-526; 571-576.
[2] Köstlin, *Martin Luther*, i, pp. 695-723.
[3] Bax, pp. 275-326.

rara avis, and that a pious one has been still rarer. Princes are usually either the greatest fools or the greatest scoundrels in the world; hence little good may be expected of them, particularly in religious matters. . . . Name a prince who is clever; pious and godly and what a marvel of God's kindness he appears to the people of the land! . . . It has come to such a pass that there are few princes who are not considered fools or knaves. . . . We may not, we will not, we can not any longer tolerate their tyranny and wickedness. . . . It is no longer to be borne, as formerly, when they drove the people about like wild beasts. Princes! Cease your wickedness; consider what is right and allow God's Word to have its way for it will have it despite yourselves. . . . A prince should not say to himself "the land and its people are mine, therefore will I do what I wish with them." He should say "I will do what is right and useful." . . . When a prince is a fool or a knave the whole country suffers.[1]

The insincerity and selfishness of princes aroused Luther's biting satire. "If these princes," he exclaimed, "had a city or a castle taken away from them by the emperor, how quickly they would rise in revolt! Yet they consider it perfectly proper to oppress the poor and put down rebellions and then say that it is by the command of the emperor. Formerly such men were called rogues, now we call them God-fearing princes."[2]

What had inspired this attack was evidently a hostile attitude on the part of some of the princes toward Luther's preaching.[3] This led him to believe the theory that the power of the government was limited to secular matters, and concerned only the lives and property of the people

---
[1] *Werke* (Weimar), xi, pp. 267 *et seq.*   [2] *Ibid.*, p. 246.

[3] In several places, particularly in Bavaria, the princes had commanded that all copies of the New Testament be given up to the authorities. Luther exhorted every one to refuse to obey this command on pain of forfeiting salvation. *Ibid.*, p. 267.

but not their souls. He warned the secular authorities to confine themselves to their proper duties and not to interfere in religious matters but "God has twisted their minds in order to make an end of them, as he did with the ecclesiastical lords."[1]

In the same pamphlet he discusses the origin and nature of government. His idea as to the origin of civil government is not different from that of Gregory VII. Luther firmly believed in the mediaeval notion that the state was not a Christian institution, but arose through man's wickedness. The real Christian needs no government, constitution or laws, but

> among a thousand people there is hardly one real Christian. People if left without government would devour each other; no one could bring up children, make a living or worship God, hence the world would soon become a desert. For these reasons two governments are instituted: the church, inspired by Christ because of the few real Christians, and the state for the wicked, and its purpose is to keep the unruly in order.[2]

This treatise on government was written during the revolt of the knights under Franz von Sickingen, and it was inferred that Luther was in secret sympathy with the movement. The Bavarian chancellor von Eck wrote: "A pamphlet has been widely distributed in which the people are exhorted to throw off the yoke of princes, kings and lords. To do this would, they are told, be acting according to what is right and just. All such things come from that wicked man Luther and from Franz von Sickingen. If ever there was a *Bundschuh* against the princes this is one."[3] Melanchthon denied

---
[1] *Werke, op. cit.*, pp. 262–265.   [2] *Ibid.*, p. 251.
[3] Jörg, *Deutschland in der Revolutionsperiode*, p. 61.

that Luther had anything to do with the revolt, and claimed that, on the contrary, he was deeply grieved over the uprising, as it hurt his cause.¹ Duke George of Saxony denounced Luther's pamphlet as scandalous, and advised the Elector Frederick to suppress it, but the latter refused to interfere.²

Yet in spite of his vehement attacks upon the princes, Luther in this very document nullifies his hostility by declaring against reform if it meant opposition to their authority.

Government should not be opposed with force but with knowledge and truth. If you succeed, well and good, but if not, then you are not to be blamed, for you suffer injustice for the sake of God. . . . If a prince does injustice, ought then his people to obey? No. To do wrong is encumbent on no one, as God not man must be obeyed. But you may ask, how is one to know whether he is in the right? If in doubt, then obey the command of the prince rather than endanger your salvation.³

A year or two earlier (1521), Luther had declared against active resistance to the authorities and had advised his own followers to desist from rioting and yield implicit obedience to the government. He evidently felt that the hostility of the princes would be fatal to his movement. In a pamphlet called *A Sincere Exhortation to all Christians to Beware of Rioting*, he says:

Rebellion never brings about reform since it does more harm to the innocent than to the guilty, hence no rebellion is right. . . . The government is founded for the purpose of punishing the wicked and protecting the good, but when *Herr Omnes*

¹ *Corpus Reform.*, i, p. 598.   ² Janssen, ii, p. 264.
³ *Werke* (Weimar), xi, p. 277.

rises, he strikes right and left and both innocent and guilty suffer; therefore obey the government in all things. If you can persuade it to change its attitude well and good; if not, obey anyway. . . . I shall always side with those who condemn rebellion and against those who cause it.[1]

Melanchthon, the bosom friend of Luther, in a letter to the Elector Palatine Ludwig, expresses the attitude of the Protestant reformers toward government even more forcibly:

For the sake of peace a Christian should be law-abiding, whatever the law may be; indeed, discontent hurts the soul's welfare. If serfdom exists, it should be left alone for the sake of peace. The Gospel does not require a change in the serf's condition, but it does require obedience to the government. . . . Whatever good is done to the government is done to God, and he who cheerfully bears burdens and taxes most truly serves God.

He goes on to say that to rebel against princes is to rebel against God; and even if a prince is a tyrant it is wrong to revolt against him as God does not desire revolution. A Christian should bear injustice patiently.[2] In his long disputes with the Anabaptists, Carlstadt and Münzer, Luther charged them with preaching open revolt against the authorities.[3] In a letter to the princes of Saxony in 1524, he declared that "the Anabaptists intend to carry through their ideas by the sword, which means that they are determined to destroy the secular power and put themselves in its place. This is against Christ, Who said that His kingdom was not of this world. . . . You, princes, must recollect that your power and authority

---

[1] *Werke* (Erlangen), xxii, p. 43.   [2] *Werke* (Walch), xvi, pp. 35-41.
[3] *Against the Heavenly Prophets*, in *Werke* (Weimar), xviii, pp. 37-215.

was given to you by God to preserve the peace. Therefore you must not sleep and be remiss in your duties."[1]

Luther's idea of attaining reform was not through revolution but through agitation, feeling certain that, if it were right, God would find some way of bringing it about in spite of the authorities. "I have often said," he declared in 1525, "and say it now, that the great battles are to be fought with the pen against the pen. The sword should be snatched from the hands of the one who wishes to use it, as he is not inspired by the Holy Spirit but is a rogue."[2] To the charge of the Catholics that he was responsible for the peasants' uprising, he defended himself by saying that everybody knew that he taught quietly and strove zealously against disorder, and had even preached obedience to tyrannical despotism. He put the blame on the "murderous prophets" who had stirred up sedition among the people, unchecked save by himself.[3]

Fundamentally Luther was a very conservative man in political and economic matters. His denunciation of princes led many to consider him a political radical and a champion of the people, whereas he was merely making a moral protest against abuses but not at all against princely authority. If a despot was cruel Luther denounced his cruelty, not his despotism. The absolute power of princes he regarded as a part of the divine order of things. It is not uncommon to find a man radical in religious matters and at the same time very conservative in matters political and economic. The very moral and religious individualism of Luther caused him

[1] *Werke* (Weimar), xv, p. 210.
[2] *A Warning Against False Prophets*, in *Werke* (Weimar), xvii, p. 364.
[3] *Ibid.*, xviii, p. 296.

to look beyond the environment for man's salvation. His general skepticism of reform he expressed later, in 1526. "Changing and bettering conditions," he declared, "are as far apart as Heaven and Earth. A change is easy enough to bring about, but to reform is dubious and dangerous, as it is not in our power but in God's to cause improvement."[1] He had a hearty contempt for the mass of people, whom he called *Herr Omnes*. Nothing was so repugnant to him as the idea that the lower classes should have something to say in the direction of human affairs. "God would prefer," he declared in a sermon of 1528 "to suffer the government to exist no matter how evil rather than allow the rabble to riot no matter how justified they are in doing so. . . . When *Herr Omnes* seizes the sword under the impression that he is doing right, then evil begins. A prince should remain a prince no matter how tyrannical he may be. He beheads necessarily only a few, since he must have subjects in order to be a ruler."[2]

Yet to the common man of Germany Luther at first appeared as a champion against oppression. His attack upon the churchmen, who were regarded as exploiters by the masses, was hailed with enthusiasm everywhere. The peasants, particularly, seemed to see in the bold monk the very man who voiced their wrongs. Hence it was to him that they came for advice and sympathy. They sent him a copy of "The Twelve Articles" and asked his opinion of their demands. In reply, Luther issued a long statement in which he discussed not only "The Twelve Articles" but government and reform in general. This pamphlet, called *An Exhortation to Peace*,

---

[1] *Werke* (Erlangen), xxii, p. 264.
[2] *Ibid.*, l, pp. 294 *et seq.*

was printed in April, 1525.[1] He begins with a warning to the princes to cease their tyranny and stop persecuting the Gospel;[2] else they must face God's retribution, now visible in the rioting of the peasants, at present only a spark, but which might yet ignite all Germany. He then addresses himself to the peasants and declares that he considers some of their articles just and reasonable; but, quoting the Bible, "For they that take the sword shall perish by the sword," Luther asserts emphatically:

No one should willfully resist authority, as St. Paul says— "Let every soul be subject unto the higher powers with fear and awe." . . . You say that the government is wicked and unbearable and destroys us body and soul. My answer is that even if princes are wicked and unjust it does not excuse rebellion. . . . The natural universal law is that no man should be his own judge . . . hence rebellion is not only against the Gospel but also against natural law and justice. . . . Can you not see that if your ideas were to prevail, every man would become the judge of his fellow? This would result in anarchy, injustice and bloodshed. If this sort of thing is not to be tolerated from one person, it certainly can not be from many, which is riot; hence both individual and mob violence is wrong. The heathen and Turks obey this divine and natural law, and if you disobey it you are worse than they, though you call yourselves Christians. What would Christ say to your calling yourselves a Christian assembly (which you are far from being) and disobeying His commands? . . . Be obedient not only to good rulers but to wicked ones. For weal or for woe, you must bear your lot in patience, for God is just and will not let you suffer long. Take care that you do not jump from the frying pan into the fire; that in trying to get bodily freedom you do not lose forever your lives, property

[1] *Werke* (Weimar), xviii, pp. 293 *et seq.*
[2] It is significant that every time Luther denounces the princes it is for persecuting the Gospel.

and souls. God's anger is aroused. So Beware! . . . You are proud of the name Christian, then listen to what Christ says— "Resist not evil." How do your ideas agree with this saying? . . . Renounce then the name Christian and call yourselves by another, or else Christ himself will tear it from you. . . . God said (Psalm 49) "Call upon me in thy need and I will help you." This is the correct Christian way of getting rid of misfortune and evil: namely, to suffer in patience and call upon God for help. Because you do not do this and depend upon your own strength, thence comes it that God does not help you.[1]

He then takes up the subject of the peasants' demands and immediately pounces on the one calling for the abolition of serfdom. To his mind the article contemplates sheer robbery and an attempt to subvert what seems to him the natural and Christian order of things. "There should be no serfs because Christ has freed us all!" he exclaims,

What is that? This means to interpret Christian freedom in an entirely material sense. Did not Abraham and other patriarchs and prophets have serfs? Read what St. Paul says about servants, who at all times have been serfs. For this reason the article is directly against the Gospel. It aims to rob the lord, who would be deprived of the serfs, his property. A serf can be a good Christian and enjoy Christian freedom just as a sick man or prisoner, though the latter is not free. This article would make all men equal and so change the spiritual Kingdom of Christ into an external worldly one. Impossible! An earthly kingdom can not exist without inequality of persons. Some must be free, others serfs, some rulers, others subjects; as St. Paul says—"Before Christ both master and slave are one."[2]

---

[1] *Werke* (Weimar), xviii, pp. 311-319.
[2] *Ibid.*, pp. 326 *et seq.* Melanchthon, too, was asked his opinion of

His solution of the problem is peace. He presents no definite plan of arbitration but asks each side to lay down its arms and come to an understanding worthy of Christians. "My advice is," he declares, "that representatives from the nobility and town councils should meet and settle this matter peacefully. You, lords, had better loosen your stiff necks a bit now for you will have to do so later whether you wish it or not. You ought to relax your oppression and tyranny and give the poor man a little air and room. On the other hand you, peasants, should give up some of your articles for they demand entirely too much."[1] He then winds up with a violent denunciation of both lords and peasants should they refuse to heed his advice. "You, lords, do not fight against Christians, for Christians do not struggle but bear all things. Your opponents are public robbers who put to shame the very name Christian and who are eternally damned. You, peasants, do not fight against

"The Twelve Articles," and his ideas on serfdom are identical with those of Luther. "It is a malicious and evil idea," he writes, "that serfdom should be abolished because Christ has made us free. This refers only to spiritual freedom given to us by Christ in order to enable us to withstand the devil. . . . A Christian may be a serf, subject, noble or prince. His condition has nothing to do with his belief. Joseph and his brethren were serfs in Egypt, as were other holy men." To the other demands of the peasants he answers "that the Germans are such a rough, obstinate, bloody-minded people, that they should be treated even more harshly than they are." *Werke* (Walch), xvi, pp. 48-50. When a nobleman asked Melanchthon's advice about removing certain burdens from his peasants, he replied: "Your lordship should not abolish the old services, and your conscience need not be troubled on this point. Discipline in bodily matters is well-pleasing to God; and if the burdens fall unequally and are too hard, we must remember what St. Paul says, 'the powers that be are ordained of God.'" Janssen, ii, p. 621.

[1] *Werke* (Weimar), xviii, p. 333.

Christians but against murderers of the Holy Spirit[1] and they too are eternally damned. Both of you now have God's judgment as I understand it."[2]

The peasants were bitterly disappointed in this reply from one who they believed would surely champion their cause. Yet Luther, powerful as he was, could not stay the rapid course of the revolutionary movement. The peasants had firmly resolved upon action and paid no heed to his advice. This evidently nettled him for we find him writing to a friend that "Peasants are no better than straw; they will not heed the Word and are without sense, hence they must bear the crack of the whip and the whiz of the bullet. . . . If they refuse to obey, let the cannon balls whistle among them, or they will make things a thousand times worse."[3]

In May, 1525, he issued a pamphlet called *Against the Thieving and Murderous Bands of Peasants*, which, for violence and brutality, is unmatched even in Luther's writings. This may be partly explained by his jealousy of Carlstadt and Münzer, whom he hated as rivals and opponents, and who were now the recognized leaders of the common people. Luther had come to regard himself as a prophet of God whose advice was the command of the Almighty Himself. And who is so apt to become enraged as a prophet flouted? He begins by saying that in his answer to the Twelve Articles he had been mild towards the peasants, who were ungrateful enough to refuse his teachings and to begin robbing and rioting like mad dogs. Their professed belief in the Gospel is only a pretext for bloodshed. It then becomes his duty to write differently concerning such miserable wretches and lay their sins before them.

[1] Persecutors of Luther's "Gospel."
[2] *Ibid.*, p. 333.
[3] De Wette, *Briefe*, ii, p. 666.

The peasants have burdened themselves with three kinds of awful sins against both God and man, for which they deserve death of body and soul. First, they had sworn to be loyal and obedient to their most gracious rulers, according to God's commands. As they have deliberately broken their allegiance, therefore have they forfeited their bodies and souls like perjured, scoundrelly wretches. . . . Sooner or later they will incur the anger of God, who desires that we should be loyal and dutiful. Secondly, they rob and destroy monasteries and castles for which, like other highwaymen and murderers, they deserve the two-fold death of body and soul. He who slays a rioter, condemned alike by the laws of God and the emperor, does what is right. Anybody may be both judge and executioner of a rioter, just as he who first puts out a fire is considered the best man. Rebellion is not merely wicked murder but a sort of general conflagration, which devastates the land, brings blood-shed and creates widows and orphans. Therefore, whoever can, should smite, strangle or stab, secretly or publicly.

Finally, he denounces the peasants for calling themselves Christians and says that they are inspired not by Christ but by the devil. In answer to the argument that Christianity means equality in person and goods, he answers: "Baptism does not make persons and property free but only the soul. . . . You, peasants, wish the property of others to be distributed and still to keep your own. What a fine lot of Christians you are! I verily believe that every devil in hell has entered your souls." He furthermore declares that any prince who refuses to put rebels to death is himself guilty of murder and robbery, but if he does punish, he can then say to God:

Behold, Thou hast called me to be a prince or lord hence I do not hesitate. Thou hast given me a sword with which to punish evil doers. . . . Therefore, dear lords, help and pity these poor folk and save them from themselves. Stab, slay and strangle wherever you can; if you are killed in this struggle, you are indeed to be felicitated, as no nobler death could befall anyone. You will die in obedience to God's Word and Command and in the service of love in trying to rescue the people from the clutches of the devil.[1]

As we have already seen, the lords were not slow in following this advice of Luther to the letter.

There was a great reaction against Luther on account of his attitude towards the uprising. The common people turned from him and his cause. "Dr. Lügner," as they now called him, was hardly a name to conjure with among the German masses. Luther deeply felt this loss of confidence and was stung into a defense of his attitude. In a letter to Casper Müller, Chancellor of Mansfeld, he stoutly refuses to yield his former position.

A rebel does not deserve to be reasoned with, but to be knocked down. The peasants refused to heed advice, so they had to heed bullets. . . . Whoever does not wish to listen quietly to God's word will listen to the executioner. I am accused of being merciless. We are not talking now of mercy but of God's word, which exalts the king and condemns the rebel, and is more merciful than we. If my words displease you, what of it? Do they not please God? When He wishes to show anger, and not mercy, why do you talk of mercy? . . . When the peasants were plundering and murdering the princes and lords, who then talked of mercy? At that time everybody shrieked "Justice! Justice! Justice!" But now when the peasants are down and the stone they threw against heaven falls on their own heads, no one talks of justice, only of mercy.

He defends his former opinions about a Christian's duty

[1] *Werke* (Weimar), xviii, pp. 357-361.

to obey the government. God may show mercy, but it is the duty of a prince to punish, as it is sometimes better to cut off one member mercilessly in order to save the whole body. Every subject should be willing to sacrifice himself for the sake of his prince. "If I were to jump between my lord and his enemy, would not that be a noble deed, praised alike by God and man? And if I were to die defending my lord, how could one ask for a death more Christian? For should I not have died in God's service?" He concludes by saying that his pamphlet against the peasants was just such an act, and in saving the lords he did the work demanded by God.[1] It is plain that under stress of circumstances Luther had worked himself into a fit of loyalty to the princes that is almost pathetic. His robust sense of humor seems entirely gone.

There are several satisfactory explanations for his hostility to the peasants' demands. In the first place, he naturally turned aside from political and economic reform, because he feared it would ruin the religious cause which he had most at heart. "It is the devil's dear wish," he had declared in 1522, "to bring about a political rebellion in order to hinder and disgrace the religious revolt."[2] He felt, and quite rightly, that his religious reforms, in order to be carried through, had to be backed up by the power of the princes or else he would meet the same fate as John Huss. How could he then take the part of the peasants whose uprising threatened vitally the interest of his protectors? Yet it is hardly fair to say that Luther deliberately acted the part of a willing tool, as his Socialist critics would have us believe. At bottom he was still to a very large extent

---

[1] *Werke* (Weimar), xviii, pp. 384-401.   [2] *Ibid.*, viii, p. 683.

a mediaeval man. While he had broken away from the Mediaeval Church, he had not at all shaken off his mediaeval psychology which was too deeply rooted to be eradicated, even in the apostle of a new Christianity. Hence his conception of man's freedom was of a purely spiritual kind. Luther wished the peasant well—that he should have plenty to eat and be comfortably housed; but he seems at times to regard any direct striving for other things than for the betterment of the soul as treason to God. The very thought of political and economic freedom seemed an intrusion upon his ideals. "Behold!" he cries at the end of his great tract, *On the Freedom of a Christian Man*, "this is the righteous, spiritual, Christian idea of freedom; that which frees the heart from sins, laws and edicts; that which overtops all other kinds of freedom, as heaven does the earth. May God give us the power to behold and understand it!"[1] Indeed, his position towards serfdom was an indication of the continued influence upon his mind of the monastic ideal of poverty and contempt for the body and for material things in general.

Luther's rejection of social reform was in harmony with the fundamental Christian idea, Protestant as well as Catholic, that man's salvation is independent of his environment. It is not the business of a Christian to better the condition of the world or himself. God's kingdom upon earth does not mean comfort and equality but the reign of personal righteousness. In fact, disadvantageous social conditions are not conceived of in Christian philosophy as a bar but as a spur to a nobler life. It seems perfectly natural and reasonable that Luther should have eyed with suspicion any scheme of

---

[1] *Werke* (Weimar), vii, p. 38.

social reform that was associated with his movement. His hostility towards the peasants was intensified by their declared adherence to the "Gospel," a claim which he indignantly regarded as a wicked subterfuge.[1] But, "they drank in with eagerness his thoughts that all were equal before God, and that there are divine commands about the brotherhood of mankind of more importance than all human legislation. They refused to believe that such golden ideas belonged to the realm of the spiritual life alone, or that the only prescriptions which denied the rights of the common man were the decrees of the Roman Curia."[2]

[1] See Art. xii, cf. *infra*, p. 142.
[2] Lindsay, i, p. 328.

PART II
SCHEMES OF REFORM

I

THE REFORMATION OF EMPEROR SIGISMUND
(CIRCA 1437)

IN the literature of reform there is no more interesting document than the Reformation of Emperor Sigismund, a typical product of mid-fifteenth century conditions, when mediaeval society was undergoing dissolution. It was undoubtedly written during the sessions of the Council of Basel when attention was being directed to reforms of all kinds.[1] For a long while it was generally believed that the emperor was the actual author or inspirer of the document. There was current in the fifteenth century in Germany, a Messianic notion that some day a great emperor-reformer would arise who would put an end to the evils of strife and sefishness and restore mankind to Christian virtue.[2] The reputation of Sigismund as a bold champion of reform caused many to believe him responsible for the "Reformation." But the absurdity of the idea of imperial authorship is made clear by the contents of the document itself. It declares for example that the emperor is a weak, unheeded person and, moreover, the rightful vassal of the pope according to the Donation of Constantine.[3]

[1] 1431-1444. The exact year in which the "Reformation" was first issued is not certain. It is generally thought to be about 1437. The only MS. copy is in the royal library of Munich.
[2] Bezold, *Geschichte der deut. Reformation*, p. 148.
[3] Goldast, *Collectio constitutionum imperialium*, iv, pp. 170, 191.

The first attempt to ascertain the true author of this remarkable manifesto was made by Goldast who included the document in one of his collections, published in 1713.[1] He promulgated the theory that a certain Friedrich von Landskron, a councillor of Sigismund, wrote the pamphlet and then issued it in the emperor's name and with his consent.[2] This was the accepted theory till 1876 when a new edition was issued by Willy Böhm together with a new theory of its authorship. Böhm identified Friedrich von Landskron with a wandering Hussite preacher named Friedrich Reiser who was burned as a heretic at Strassburg in 1458. Reiser, according to Böhm, was the real writer of the "Reformation."[3]

Böhm's suggestion aroused general discussion. W. Bernhardi, in a review of the book, flatly denied the possibility that a Hussite could have been the author, since the pamphlet explicitly declares that the pope is the protector of the Christian faith and supreme over the emperor;[4] Reiser, according to Böhm, had stigmatized the pope as no higher than a wicked layman.[5] Vogt compromised by saying it was "Hussite in political and economic matters but Catholic in religion."[6] Bezold, a great authority on the Hussite movement, was of the

[1] Goldast, iv, pp. 170-200. Goldast divided the document into two parts, religious (pp. 170-188) and secular (pp. 188-200). The first edition of the pamphlet appeared in 1476, published in Augsburg by Johannes Bämler. *Chroniken der deutsche Städte*, viii, pp. 192, 217. Three succeeding editions appeared in Augsburg, 1480, 1484 and 1497. During 1520-21 four or five more editions were issued, the most important of which was that by Thoman Wolff of Basel. Böhm, *Friedrich Reisers Reformation des Kaisers Sigismund*, pp. 5-20.

[2] *Coll. cons. imp.*, iv, p. 170.   [3] Böhm, pp. 50-95.

[4] Jenaer Litteraturzeitung (1876), pp. 792 et seq.

[5] Böhm, p. 90.

[6] Vogt, *Vorgeschichte des Bauernkrieges*, p. 72.

opinion that the author of the "Reformation" was not a Hussite, but a far more conservative reformer who accepted church and state as traditionally organized.[1] Recently an entirely new view has been put forth; namely, that the author was neither a priest nor a Hussite, but the town notary of some imperial city in southwestern Germany, because a special appeal is made to the imperial towns to undertake the cause of reform.[2]

At present the question of the authorship of the "Reformation" is still in the province of speculation. Whoever he may have been, he certainly was not Emperor Sigismund. It is not improbable that the "Reformation" was the work of some obscure individual who issued it in the name of Sigismund with the pious hope that the emperor would be willing to play the role of reformer. The document is unfortunately too long to be reproduced here in full, but the summary which follows will, it is hoped, give an adequate notion of its contents.[3]

The opening paragraph of this famous scheme is intoned in the true medieval style of moral and religious emotion. "Oh God!" it exclaims, "we wander about in Thy pastures without Thy leave. Obedience is dead and justice is in distress.

> Deviat ab ordine totum quod movetur ;
> Labitur, exoritur, viribus doletur.

It is certain that all will not be well with us until we bring about a righteous re-organization of the spiritual and temporal powers, which at present rest on evil foundations." The imperial cities are exhorted to take

---
[1] Bezold, *Zur deutschen Kaisersage*, pp. 586 *et seq.*
[2] Koehne, *Studien zur sogennanten Reformation Kaiser Sigmunds.*
[3] The text used is in Goldast, *Collectio cons. imp.*, iv, pp. 170-200.

up the work of reform as they are the only element vigorous and righteous enough to do it; the lords being evil, the emperor powerless and the empire sick, tottering and weak.

The secular part of the pamphlet begins with a complaint that there are too many taxes. There ought to be only one, because the original purpose of taxation was for roads and bridges. Hence there should be none levied except for these purposes, and "he who levies taxes with which he does not build roads should be held up to public scorn as a sinner and usurer." Those lords who insist on collecting them should be openly attacked. The clergy are to be exempt from all taxation. Each city is to appoint a commission of two men whose duties it shall be to regulate tolls and the building of roads and bridges.[1]

The guilds should be abolished because of their insolence, exclusiveness and corruption. The guildmasters, through their power in the town councils, have become a source of tyranny and oppression. A vigorous complaint is made against a man's being in more than one trade and so infringing on another's business, which is against law and custom. A vintner sells salt or cloth; a tailor becomes a merchant as well. The government should prevent such practices by heavy fines.

Then an attack is made on the dishonesty of merchants. The author charges them with making secret agreements to raise prices. He suggests that imperial officials should be stationed in every part of the land to whom sworn statements shall be made of the cost price of every article. The government, too, should regulate the selling

[1] Goldast, *op. cit.*, p. 188.

price. Then follows a bitter denunciation of the great companies who "do evil to the common welfare of both city and country." These monopolies must be rooted out. If a member is a burgher, his entire stock should be confiscated, and if a noble he should be degraded from his rank. A commission should be appointed to regulate the prices of domestic goods and the wages of day laborers.

Serfdom is bitterly denounced as an abomination in the sight of a Christian. "It is a thing of unheard-of wickedness which ought to awaken all Christendom, that there are some people who can say to others, 'you belong to me.' Why then has Christ died for us? Was it not in order to make us free and loosen our bonds so that one should not be above another? All who are baptized,—noble and commoner, rich and poor—are equal and belong to the body of Christ."[1] "Sad to say, even monasteries have serfs. They pretend to be Christian, but have fallen away from God. I wish to say emphatically that he who wants to remain a Christian must not have serfs. Destruction should be the portion of those who refuse to free those they hold." The writer then proceeds to attack the monks as the enemies of the poor and usurpers of political power.[2]

A bitter attack is made on the lords for first confiscating the common lands and then taxing the peasants for the right to use them. "They transgress the peasant's rights and live on his labor." Game laws should be totally abolished. "Sad to relate, things have come to such a pass that if the lords could dominate the entire earth and sea they would do so." Such a condition of affairs calls for the heavy vengeance of God.[3]

[1] Goldast, *op. cit.*, p. 191.   [2] *Ibid.*, p. 191.   [3] *Ibid.*, p. 191.

Every city is to have a physician salaried by the government who is to treat everybody without charge. A body curer is as essential as a soul curer. Physicians should know particularly the anatomy of the brain and liver, the two sources of all illness. The current coinage is denounced as false in weight and quality, from which result all kinds of evil and fraud. Counterfeiters should be punished by burning at the stake. All private concessions to coin money should be withdrawn and new coins issued bearing on one side the imperial stamp and on the other the arms of those persons who, after a thorough investigation, are granted the right to coin money. The "Reformation" then closes with a violent attack on the mendicant orders.

It is difficult for a modern man to analyze accurately any intellectual product of the Middle Ages. The lack of a critical sense so characteristic of the writers of that period resulted in a confusion of thought that makes any attempt to gauge the true significance of a document like this one a hopeless task. The mediaeval man had an *idée fixe*. religion, which entered as a blend into all his thoughts, political, economic, scientific or artistic. This "Reformation" is a strange mixture of radicalism and conservatism, of democracy and autocracy, of heresy and orthodoxy. It demands the abolition of serfdom on the ground of natural human equality, yet it provides for a caste system by which a man was to be permanently confined to one sort of work. According to Lamprecht, the author is the democratic spokesman of the lower classes in town and country.[1] Böhm considers him the special champion of the lower

[1] Lamprecht, *Zum Verständniss der wirtschaftlichen u. socialen Wandlungen in Deutschland*, p. 218.

town-workers against the arrogance of the guild-masters.[1] Yet he recognizes class distinctions, as for example, in meting out different punishments to burgher and knight. Throughout, there is also a most rigid adherence to the mediaeval ideas of pope and emperor. Nevertheless, the Reformation of Emperor Sigismund is a document of prime importance in the history of the peasant uprisings in Germany. Its energetic espousal of the secular demands of the common people, couched in vivid phraseology, was a powerful influence for discontent. It was the first to sound the demand for "God's Justice," which became the battle cry of the great revolt of 1525. During the years 1520–1525 it was very widely circulated. The Reformation of Emperor Frederick III and the Divine Evangelical Reformation of Hipler are directly modeled on it.[2] The "Reformation" directly or indirectly became the inspiration of all those who were seeking to overthrow the intolerable tyranny of hierarchy, feudal lords and monopolists.

[1] Böhm, p. 44.   [2] *Cf. infra*, pp. 104, 128.

II

THE REFORMATION OF EMPEROR FREDERICK III
(CIRCA 1523)

Introduction

ALONG with the Reformation of Emperor Sigismund, there appeared another document expressing similar ideas, known under the title of the Reformation of Emperor Frederick III. Like the former, it too sprang from an unknown source, and has left scholarship to conjecture its authorship. The scheme has been popularly ascribed to the Emperor Frederick III (IV) who was supposed to have issued it as a sort of charter of liberties in the year 1441. This theory is manifestly improbable. The document contains strikingly bold criticisms of the clergy and of the upper ranks of nobility, as well as of the administration of law and the system of taxation. It is evidently the work of a fervid reformer. But the Emperor Frederick III was never known to have interested himself in any radical reform measures. His long reign (1440-1493) is filled with petty wars with the Swiss, Hungarians and the Austrian nobles. The main interest of his life seems to have been to increase his family domains; his most striking achievement was the marriage of his son Maximilian to the daughter of Charles the Bold. Moreover, the "Reformation" is not to be found among the official documents of Frederick's reign, which were first published under the title of *Neue Sammlung der Reichsabschieden*. Frederick's supposed authorship gained currency through its advocacy by G. W. Böhmer, an early nineteenth-century liberal, who stoutly maintained that the emperor was a sort of Joseph II.[1] Goldast's theory is that the pamphlet emanated from the councils of the imperial towns and was presented by their representatives to the emperor at an imperial diet in 1441.[2] This is hardly possible, because Article XI is distinctly opposed to the business interests of the great trading centers. Besides, the whole scheme of judicial re-organization proposed in Article VII is too much in the direction of centralization to have suited the interests of the great cities, whose autonomy, guaranteed by special privileges, would have been threatened by a plan which proposed to give representation to all the estates of the empire—even to the communes and provincial towns. In fact, it is quite impossible that the document could have been written at all during the reign of Frederick III. The bitter complaint against the doctors of the law, contained in Article V, could not have been made in the middle of the fifteenth century when there were but few Roman lawyers in the service of the cities and princes.[3]

The "Reformation" appears to be the work of a religious enthusiast, who had the ideas of political, judicial and economic reform that agitated Germany during the Protestant Revolt. Throughout, there is an identity of phraseology as well as of thought with the peasant manifestos of 1525. The plan of Hipler, as given by Oechsle, bears so striking a resemblance to it, that it seems evident that Hipler took the document as his model.[4] Ranke

[1] Böhmer, *Friedrich III. Entwurf einer Magna Charta für Deutschland*, pp. 1-20.
[2] Goldast, *Reichssätzungen*, i, p. 392.   [3] *Cf. infra*, p. 128.
[4] Oechsle, *Beiträge zur Gesch. des Bauernkriegs*, p. 163.

declares that "it breathes the spirit of the first years of the Reformation."¹ In the opinion of Eichhorn, the probable author was Thomas Münzer, the peasant leader of Thuringia, because he was in Zwickau in 1523, the place and date of the first printed edition of the work.² This, however, is obviously not conclusive reasoning. Moreover, had Münzer been the author, the document would have been couched in more radical language and would have emphasized the demands of the peasants, which it does not. Jörg's idea is that it was gotten up by Von Hutten in the interest of the Sickingen party.³ This is improbable, as Article XII, abolishing the collection of tolls, is too directly opposed to the interests of the knightly order, which Von Hutten represented. In all probability, the "Reformation" was a species of "pious fraud," perpetrated by some unknown reformer of the early Protestant period.⁴

¹ Ranke, ii, p. 203.
² Eichhorn, *Deutsche Staats- und Rechtsgeschichte*, iii, § 408.
³ Jörg, p. 302.
⁴ The following editions are known:
(a) There are only two copies of the earliest edition. One is at the Royal Library at Munich. Panzer, *Annalen*, nos. 2062, 2063. It consists of twenty unnumbered pages with the date 1523 printed on the first page. The names of the place and printer are missing. The title in full reads: "Teütscher Nationnodturfft. Die Ordnung unnd Reformation aller Stend im Römischer Reich. Durch Keyser Fridrich den driten Gott zû lob, der gantzen Christenheit zû nutz und seligkeyt fürgenomen." The other copy was in the possession of C. G. Homeyer (*Monatsber. der k. pr. Akad. der Wissen.* (1856), p. 296). It bears no date and has the same title as the above, with the following addition: "Gedruckt zû Zwickaw durch Jorg Gastel des Schonsperger diener von Augspurg."
(b) The "Exempel und Inquisition der Papisten und Jesuiten" of Philon von Trier, printed in 1607, contains the plan under the following title: "K Friderici III Reformation, von Nothdurft Teuscher Nation, als dieser zeit hochnothwendig inseriret .... Jetzo auf's neue

The main source of the Reformation of Frederick III was undoubtedly the Reformation of Kaiser Sigismund. Was it the purpose of the author of the new "Reformation" to present a scheme of social re-organization along democratic lines? A careful perusal of the document will convince anyone who does not read into it the radicalism of the nineteenth and twentieth centuries that it was not. It was, rather, the moral protest of a religious reformer of the Lutheran period against certain evils of his day. The proposals for reform are moderate enough: honest coinage, abolition of tolls, regulation of the merchants' associations and the substitution of the old German law for the newer Roman law. There are lacking in this program the comprehensiveness of Geismayr's plan as well as the definite peasant demands of the Twelve Articles. Nowhere is there found any article distinctly in the interest of the lower classes in town or country. The value of the document lies in the fact that like the Reformation of Emperor Sigismund it, too, furnished a convenient basis for more constructive schemes of reform.

überschen, an vielen Orten angirt, corrigirt, vermehrt und gebessert sammt einer Vorrede Aegidii Hunii." Philon's edition is vitiated by his strong anti-clerical tendency, which finds expression in violent additions to those articles directed against the clergy.

(c) The "Reformation" is to be found in a fair form in Goldast's collection, under the title "Deutscher Nation Nothdurft." Goldast acknowledges his debt to Philon von Trier, but declares that he saw the original copy in Mainz, which he says, was printed at Zwickaw in 1523. (Goldast, 166–180.)

(d) The most recent edition, based on that of Goldast, was published by G. W. Böhmer under the title: *Friedrich III. Entwurf einer Magna Charta für Deutschland* (Göttingen, 1818). It is from this edition that the following English translation is made.

[TEXT]

The Needs of the German Nation. The Reformation of all Ranks in the Roman Empire, through the Emperor Frederick III who (praised be the Lord!) was chosen for the Needs and Happiness of all Christendom.

I Every member of the clergy in the entire Roman Empire of the German Nation, shall be assigned to his proper duties without reference to birth, descent, influence, intellectual ability, or any other qualification. He shall be appointed for the exclusive purpose of serving God and shall be maintained in poverty, in order that the religion of Christ may be accepted by the common man.

The vast host of monks, priests, nuns, friars and other beggars desire to deceive the world under an appearance of holiness, with the result that the burgher in the city and the poor man in the country are so bitterly oppressed that their wives and children are often in want of daily food, in order that these lazy useless folk be sustained. If one refuses to support them, the soldiers are sent to take away his cows and calves. Sometimes in order to appear kind, they have him put under the ban, which causes him still greater harm. This is an example of their priestly mercy and Christian love. What should be given them for the love of God, they seize by tyrannical methods, all because of avarice.

II All princes in the Roman Empire of the German Nation, whether of high or low rank and all their counts, freemen, lords, and knights, and the nobles who have been created by the empire should, each and all, maintain their position according to their rank, and conduct themselves according to the laws of the empire.

Each lord shall know his place and his duties, in order that the poor men of the land shall not be oppressed, and that freedom shall be preserved.

Laws should be enacted to help each and every widow and orphan, so that no one shall be without justice.

III All free, imperial and royal cities and other communes

and communities in the Holy Roman Empire of the German Nation, shall be granted, each and all, their just rights and proper government, without regard to their ancient privileges, customs or rank, but in accordance with the principles of Christian freedom, human nature and common-sense, as interpreted by the sense of justice and natural reason of all human beings. From these the common welfare must take its beginning.

In these days the world considers selfishness as wisdom, and the common welfare is forgotten; but the latter cannot be put aside but must be considered.

IV All princes, from the Emperor to the lowest in rank, as well as counts, lords, knights and nobles, similarly the clergy of all ranks, as well as the cities and communes, all that are recognized as belonging to the Roman Empire of the German Nation, shall each have its own regulations or constitutions according to the necessities of each. They shall not be subjected to burdens.

No doctors of law, canon or civil, shall, in the light of this Reformation, be tolerated in the Roman Empire of the German Nation. They shall not be permitted in any court, or allowed to engage in any law suit or be advisors in royal and other councils but shall be entirely suppressed. Henceforth they shall not be allowed to plead, write or advise in the courts. Since God has blessed and provided each man with his own wisdom, so according to this new constitution, every man, if he so desires, shall act as his own attorney.

At each of the universities, there shall be maintained three doctors of law, whose duty it shall be to foster those laws that have been established on a true foundation. The doctors are expected to read and study only laws of this nature, and they must not permit themselves to be led beyond what is clearly decreed and demanded by the laws of the empire. When in case of doubt, and advice equivalent to a decision is asked of them, these three doctors should together examine the matter and render a decision within a month; for an unjust delay in law does great harm to the livelihood of the common man. The door of Justice at present is even more tightly shut to the doctors than to the laity; and no key can now be found till both parties in a case have become poor or are entirely ruined. The layman himself has the key to the door of Justice, and at the right moment can unlock it and bring forth righteousness. For the following reasons we cannot tolerate the learned in the courts as they are merely paid hirelings.

The doctors of the law permit all justice to remain useless and impotent; therefore are they the step-fathers and not the rightful parents of righteousness. They take away from the law the ground-work of truth; and because of their great avarice, the law is held in such contempt and discredit that no godly man will any longer put faith in it. To such a pass has your perverted learning come during the fifty years it has ruled! Have such things ever been heard of before?

It shall be permitted to all the ranks of the Roman Empire of the German nation—princes, counts, barons, lords, cities and communities—to maintain doctors of law, but with such restraints and regulations as will keep them out of all diets, where they act as attorneys and administrators. In this and other ways, they shall be restrained from influencing the councils of princes or of cities. If the doctors are expressly desired by princes or cities, then they shall be permitted to hold advisory consultations before which only important cases shall be tried. They shall not be permitted to learn the secrets of the prince or of the city that employs them, because they do not keep silent about anything. Such councillors act merely for the sake of pay and from motives of avarice.

VI No priests, henceforth, whether of high or low rank, shall ever sit in the secular councils of the emperor, princes, counts, lords, cities or communes, either as members or advisors. It is not seemly for them to meddle in secular matters, no matter how strongly they desire to do so, for many weighty reasons, all of which it is not necessary to enumerate here. Because of their meddling in secular affairs:

(1) The worship of God is discontinued.

(2) They neglect the ministry of God and depend more upon worldly honors and gifts.

(3) They set secret inquiries on foot concerning the laity, their property, friendship and animosities. They use this knowledge to enhance their own authority and turn the princes, counts and lords into their servants and serfs. The great prelates, abbots and monks have compelled the lay orders to act as guests and servants in their own households, while they (the clergy) have become the lords. This result is due to the fact that the laity have failed to keep their affairs secret from the priests who are admitted into their innermost councils. When have the clergy ever invited you to participate in their assemblies? For this and other important reasons, you were blinded and betrayed.

(4) Then, again, in reference to their great pride. If the prelates were permitted to sit in secular councils we could never come to a definite understanding as to the common welfare, which is always opposed to their pride and self-interest. Therefore, in order to bring about good government, we must expel the clergy from the councils of the emperor and of the princes. What is sin to them is not so to us and vice versa. If the priest take to himself a wife, it is wrong for him but right for us laymen; but for a priest to take away the wife of a pious man is not considered wicked, yet it is a sin for a layman to do the same thing. If a layman takes five per cent interest, it is sinful, but not so for a cleric to take sixty or seventy per cent. Either we are not Christians or they are heretics; then is our religion quite confused and contradictory. In conclusion, let me say, their pretentions are without foundation.

VII All imperial civil laws that have obtained in the Holy Roman Empire of the German Nation till now, shall be declared null and void. Only those laws that are considered, by those who know, to have their foundation in pure reason and clear truth, shall be preserved and maintained; so it will be brought to pass that the poor shall have as much free access to the laws as the rich. If a person be a prince, he should conduct himself without cunning and fraud.

(a) The *Kammergericht* shall be composed of sixteen highly honorable men. They shall choose as their president a count or lord who is also a member of the Imperial Court. The membership of this body shall be composed of two princes, two counts, two lords, two knights, three representatives from the imperial cities and four from all the communes and communities in the entire Holy Roman Empire. From this body of sixteen members, all plaintiffs and defendants may choose their advisors and advocates to take care of their cases. No one shall be admitted to membership in this court who has not formerly served for nine years as judge in his manor or commune.

(b) Below the *Kammergericht* there shall be four *Hofgerichte*. The princes, counts and lords shall appoint three members in each of these courts; the knights and vassals, three; the imperial cities, three; the princely cities, three; and all the commons and communities of the empire, four. Together, they shall choose one of themselves to act as president. These courts shall sit at all times. From these bodies, all plaintiffs and defendants shall choose their advocates and advisors to handle their cases. Every one of these judges should have had experience in courts or councils.

(c) There shall be sixteen *Landgerichte*, four under each *Hofgericht* of the empire. Each of these courts shall also consist of sixteen judges; four, representing the princes, counts and lords; four, the knights and vassals; four, the cities; and four, the communes and communities. Each of these courts shall choose as their president a man of knightly rank. There shall be uniform practice in all the courts. Two pleas shall be allowed to the plaintiff and three to the defendant; provided that in the summing up no new matter be introduced.

(d) There shall be sixty-four *Freigerichte*, four under each *Landgericht*. Like the other courts, these shall consist of sixteen members each; four from the imperial cities; four from the nobility; four from the cities whose lords are princes; and four from all the communes and communities. A nobleman shall be president of each of these courts; the same methods shall obtain in these as in the others. All city and country courts shall conduct themselves righteously.

No appeals shall be made from any of these local courts in cases involving less than ten gulden. If, however, a question of honor or inheritance be involved, then such appeals may be allowed. No appeals shall be made from any of the *Landgerichte* in cases involving a hundred gulden or less; from the *Hofgerichte*, a thousand gulden or less. In cases involving a thousand gulden or over, appeals may be taken to the *Reichskammergericht*. In these courts only, shall imperial laws, founded on truth, be enforced in the spirit of this constitution.

VIII All revenues, excises, transit duties, license dues, taxes and other similar exactions, which have existed till now in the Holy Roman Empire of the German nation, shall be entirely abolished except those that are considered necessary. Selfish interests shall no longer impose burdens on the common welfare. No obstacles shall henceforth be put in the way of commerce and trade.

Not only do the princes, counts and lords, but also the prelates, cities, communes, simple knights and vassals daily levy taxes, excises, dues and exactions of all sorts and so overload the common man that he is forced to bestir himself and throw off your evil rule. Look to it that your patrimonies are not taken away and that you are not deprived also of your lives. In truth, princes, you are on the hunt for unrighteous wealth and mean to draw the sweat and blood from the common man. This is, indeed, enough. You are warned. Where now, pray, are those eminent advisors who should inspire you to act for the general welfare? In your councils there are many flatterers, hypocrites and parasites, because you do not tolerate the truth. If any one succeeds in getting more for you through oppressing the poor, he is called a clever fellow, and no one asks whether it has come about righteously or not. As though God created his people to be your fools! Had you real Christian feelings you would think better of God's creatures. Henceforth no impositions shall be levied, other than those needed for water and land improvement; namely, bridges, paths and highways. Only when there is pressing need shall taxes be paid and not otherwise. Bridges, paths and highways shall be constructed and carefully maintained. If this be not done, the driver may rightly withhold his payment of toll till it is done.

Each tax-collector shall give an account to his superior once a year only. Whatever money he uses for building bridges, paths and highways, shall be regarded as being properly expended; and what is left shall be put in the treasury till it is needed for the common welfare. In such matters the princes should seek not their own interest but the general good.

No excise shall be laid on wine, beer, mead or other liquors, unless good reasons are given and accepted. For to-day self-interest prevails to such an extent in the government, that the authorities will not willingly allow revenue to be reduced in any way. If you knew as much as I, you would readily yield to the general good, because honorable dealing will benefit you more than evil, sinful wastefulness.

IX All concessions to coin gold and silver in the Holy Roman Empire of the German Nation shall be withdrawn without compensation. Inasmuch as the needs of the empire are general, and because there has been hitherto so much confusion, therefore all the lawful coins in the empire shall bear one stamp made by the legal imperial mint. Furthermore, the coins shall not be circulated unless they have uniform value and weight and are accepted in all exchanges. For this reason, the mines shall be free from taxation.

In the entire empire there shall be only twenty-one persons empowered to coin money. The coins shall bear the imperial eagle on one side and the coat-of-arms of the issuer on the other.

X All weights, measures, yard-sticks, etc. in the Holy Roman Empire of the German Nation shall be collected and adjusted according to the needs of the people. The wine measure shall be the same size in all places. The corn measure shall be the weight of a man's burden with which he can climb up a flight of stairs. Woolens, linens, fustian and all goods that are measured by a yardstick shall all have one length.

XI All dealing in merchandise in the entire Holy Roman Empire of the German Nation shall be reformed for the welfare of the community. The great associations, corporations and other dealers in merchandise, daily oppress the people. It is not only the nobles and prelates who complain of them but also those who deal in a small way and who have to buy all their wares from them. I will say nothing about the poor craftsmen, who buy every commodity they need at the highest prices, and are forced to sell to these associations and other merchants at the very lowest prices.

No one shall deal in more than one kind of merchandise. No merchant, alone or in partnership, shall henceforth carry on business for more than ten thousand Rhenish gulden. If he possess a larger capital, he must loan it to the government at four per cent; and the latter shall in turn loan it to the poor at five per cent.

XII All imperial roads in the Holy Roman Empire of the German Nation shall be free from tolls. In the entire land no union, alliance, secret understanding or conspiracy shall be formed; all existing ones shall be dissolved. Protection and freedom shall be sought only under the Holy Roman Empire.

In accordance with this constitution, no one shall demand or receive an escort no matter where he goes, whether he travels on land or sea, by horse or on foot. The same conditions shall hold good for his merchandise whether it is in ships or in wagons. The estates of the empire, in view of their princely privileges, feudal rights, regalia, etc. shall take all the roads under their care, with the obligation that all routes shall be kept free and safe and that they allow no traveller to be harmed. This article of the constitution is to be specially indicated and emphatically impressed upon their minds in order that the princes shall do their duty most zealously. When such duties are neglected, great harm will surely come to them. Whoever travels through the entire empire, be he stranger or native-born, his life, property and friends must be as safe as if he were in the land of his own lord. Wherever this condition shall not obtain, the domain shall be punished by fines and shall fall into the greatest disfavor in the Holy Roman Empire. This constitution provides the means to compel obedience even from the most powerful. The empire need not worry about it either, as at all times it has had its special commission to take care of such matters. The main purpose of an imperial constitution is to promote the welfare of the poor in particular and of the community in general.

All ranks shall be commanded to improve constantly the old roads, paths, and highways, as well as to construct new ones. Therefore, as it was said above, only moderate tolls and customs shall be collected. The princes, lords and all the other ranks are so well endowed with fiefs and privileges that such extortion is no longer necessary. As they do not wish to trust God, and are still less willing to trust man, it is high time that the power of God be shown in order to compel them to do their duty. They will, then, perhaps learn to know their obligations.

The purpose of these twelve articles is to provide for the good of every rank as well as for the common welfare, in order that the constitution, statutes and privileges shall remain effective and valid, that the pious shall be assisted in their labors, the widows and orphans protected, all roads made free to everybody, the wicked punished and the Christian religion maintained in brotherly love and triumph.

All obedient subjects of the empire shall compel obedience on the part of the disobedient, and at the same time accept whatever the laws of the empire impose, in order that human freedom according to Christian rule be re-established. This freedom, because of the influence of anti-Christ, has been limited and suppressed to the disadvantage of us poor Christians, as is foretold by the Holy Gospel and the other words of Christ. But through God's mercy the blind see and the dumb speak.

The following is a plan for the general military organization of the empire. There shall be at all times five large garrisons, one in the interior and four on the frontiers. Over each, there shall be a commander with a powerful battery of artillery using iron shot. A general shall command the entire corps—horse, foot and artillery. His duty shall be to suppress any discontent or discord. The four commanders on the frontier shall do likewise, in order to maintain peace and quiet in the land.

Oh ye noble Christians of low and high degree whom God has gathered in the Holy Roman Empire! Take ye notice of God's mercy which He has so graciously shown in our days. He has opened for us the treasure of His divine grace; if we refuse to praise and thank Him, we are not worthy of being called Christians. It is as plain as day that the clergy, with their smooth and cunning words, have robbed us of our rightful inheritance. It is they who have beguiled our forefathers into purchasing the Kingdom of Heaven with their paternal estates. As though the Kingdom of God could be bought for those very things which He gives us for the purpose of making our daily living! They have basely betrayed us and our forebears by using sweet words to squeeze from us money which should have gone to the support of our families. Now that we no longer have so much property and are not willing to give them any gifts, they still dare, through quarrels and even open conflicts, to take away the little property we have left and reduce us by force to abject beggary.

Consider well, Oh pious Christians, nobles and commoners, rich and poor, old and young, and take seriously to heart, whether such a state of affairs can any longer be tolerated and endured.

I should very much like to know to whom the great number of monks are of any use. Those wives and daughters that please them, they take away and turn into prostitutes. I should like to hear from anyone who knows, if Christ, our Deliverer, when he was on earth, ever said anything about monks or nuns? To whom are such people useful? The priests openly carry on their evil doings without shame or fear and no one punishes them. The monks and nuns do evil secretly, but our age will not tolerate it. There is no use in defending yourselves against these things, as we know your rascality far better than you imagine.

Return to the poor, to the needy and to the chosen children of God, the patrimony which you owe them and which has been given you by God, for He may then, perchance, have mercy upon you. Should you prefer to share it with your prostitutes and bastards rather than with the children of God to whom you rightfully owe it, be assured then, that God will reward you according to your deserts, for you have oppressed and burdened everybody in the empire. The time has now come when your property, like that of an enemy, will be taken away and distributed. Because you have oppressed the people, they will rise against your authority and you will have no place in which to abide. Only after these things have taken place, will the above twelve articles open an era of rightful government and reformation.

III

A New Organization of the Secular State, by Eberlin (Circa 1521)

Introduction

JOHAN EBERLIN VON GÜNZBURG was for a long time a neglected personality of the Protestant Revolution, until the work of his biographers, Riggenbach and Radlkofer, in the latter part of the nineteenth century, awakened an interest in him. The labors of both are, however, of a purely narrative order, with extended citations from Eberlin's writings, and they make no attempt to offer a critical study of the man and his work.

Eberlin was born in Günzburg on the Danube about the year 1470. Of his early life little is known. In 1490 we find him *magister* in the University of Basel. A few years later, he entered the Franciscan Order, and in 1519 he received the appointment as preacher in a Franciscan monastery at Tübingen.[1] He was known as an enthusiastic champion of the Church and particularly of his Order. "Those of the people," he later wrote, "who heard me preach, always heard me praise the Rule of St. Francis. At one time I spent a whole hour explaining the Third Article of the Rule." He goes on to describe his midnight vigils, fasts and self-torture as proof of his loyalty to Church and Order.[2] His strong argumentative nature drove him into quarrel-

---

[1] Radlkofer, *Joh. Eberlin von Günzburg*, p. 4.
[2] Riggenbach, *Johan Eberlin von Günzburg*, p. 12.

some debates with the learned men of Tübingen, with the result that he was transferred to Ulm as *Lesemeister*.

Eberlin's breaking away from the Church was largely due to the influence of a physician of Ulm, named Rychard, who was a great admirer of Martin Luther. In an address to the citizens of Ulm in 1523, Eberlin said, "I was a daily student of Doctor Martin Luther, and through him I was taught to preach the truth."[1]

He left his order in 1521 and became a wandering preacher and pamphleteer. We next hear of him in Switzerland as a violent agitator against priests, monks and nuns.[2] His former devotion to the Church had changed into bitter hatred. Janssen quotes him as saying that "all consecrated individuals, monks, nuns and priests, the whole lot of them, are marked with the devil's hand."[3] His preaching was forbidden by the Swiss towns, and he was driven from place to place till he fled to Wittenberg where he became associated with Luther.

Eberlin's attitude towards the Peasants' Revolt was typical of the Lutheran Reformer. When a mob of peasants appeared before the gates of the city of Erfurt where he was then residing, the authorities appealed to him to use his influence to quiet them. He came before the peasants and warned them against rioting, as such conduct disgraced the Gospel. He continually counseled patience and obedience to the authorities and denounced the authors of the Twelve Articles as cunning rascals who were misleading simple people.[4]

In a widely circulated pamphlet, *Warnung an die Christen in der Burgauischen Mark*, he says: "Your [i. e. the peasants'] lord, the devil, knows that God never allows revolution to go unpunished. That is the

[1] Radlkofer, *op. cit.*, p. 10.   [2] *Ibid.*, p. 11.
[3] Janssen, ii, p. 199.   [4] Radlkofer, p. 509.

reason why the former uprisings (*Bundschuhe*) were unsuccessful.... Tyranny rules because of God's anger, and revolt is therefore a very poor way of getting your desires."[1] He goes on to say that all evil comes from misinterpreting the Bible, which people take to promise a future equality of goods and absence of authority. "Luther has taught us that we are like prisoners before a stern Judge, who have been released through the death of His Son; therefore all faithful believers should suffer hardships and death with patience. ... From the Gospel, you know that all suffering comes from God. You ask then, how long is tyranny to exist? My answer is, as long as God wishes. ... God will not permit the common man to revolt against authority under the mask of Christian principles. ... He will destroy you as He did the worshippers of Baal."[2]

Eberlin's scheme is valuable rather for sharp criticism than for radical proposals of reform. It is naïve and theoretical in character and shows no real grasp of any political or economic problems. It is more interesting than important. Even as a theoretical scheme, it lacks unity and shows no fundamental conception of the state. It represents in a clear, forcible style, a series of detached thoughts on the lesser evils of the time, with the Lutheran note sounding throughout. Not a word is to be found about relieving the burdens of the peasants with the exception of the article declaring a common right to game, fish and forest.[3]

[1] Radlkofer, p. 531.   [2] *Ibid.*, p. 533.
[3] The following translation is taken from a reprint of the "15 Bundesgenossen" in *Neudrucke deutscher Litteraturwerke des XVI und XVII Jahrhunderts*, vol. cxvi, pp. 122-131. The first edition was probably printed in Basel in the year 1521, though it bore no date, publisher, author or place. Toward the end of one of his pamphlets, entitled *Der 7 Pfaffen Trost*, Eberlin says: "We desire also that you read with care our first fifteen pamphlets printed in Basel in 1521."

[Text]

A new Organization of the Secular State which, as Psitacus shows, was written in Wolfaria.[1]

In the eleventh Bundgenoss[2] I desire to lay before you the plan, which Psitacus says, the rulers of Wolfaria had considered in their attempts to re-organize the secular government. As yet they have not definitely accepted it because in that land, a constitution for the cities and country must first have the approval of the people in every district before it can go into effect. Yet I will not withhold from you the new proposals.

No calling shall be considered more honorable than agriculture. Even the nobles must sustain themselves by it.

In each village, there should be a nobleman possessing as much land as two plows can cultivate, and he shall be chosen mayor of the place. All the villages contained in two hundred manors shall have a knight acting as bailiff. Every month he shall call an assembly consisting of all the mayors and representative yeoman from every village to listen to the complaints of the tenants.

Every county (*Vogtei*) shall govern itself. Each proposal must be ratified by the people of the county in order to become a law; every man shall be entitled to vote.

Every city shall have ten counties under its jurisdiction. If it has not this number, it shall be called a manor, not a city.

Every manor shall have a lord who must be a baron.

The head of a city must be a count.

Every ten cities shall have over them a chief who must be either a duke or a prince.

No lord shall have power to do anything without the help and advice of an organized assembly of the people.

---

[1] An imaginary commonwealth, like Utopia.

[2] Fraternal constitution.

Each manor, city or principality shall have the right to maintain self-government.

One amongst the princes shall be known as king who shall not be permitted to do anything without the help and advice of the princes.

No mayor, bailiff, baron, count, prince or king shall hold any other office. Their services shall consist in furthering the common welfare; they shall be paid by the community according to the importance of their work.

None of the above mentioned officials shall maintain any law court other than that pertaining to his office, except such courts as are necessary for his own household.

In case an officer needs assistance to maintain the common welfare, his subordinates must put their lives and property at his service, provided he is, at all times, the first to be willing to do likewise.

All councils shall consist of as many nobles as peasants.

We ordain that all public violators of the marriage-vows shall be put to death.

None of the above-mentioned offices shall be hereditary; but in case a friend, son, or father of the incumbent is chosen by the tenants, then it shall be permitted.

All drunkards shall be drowned.

He who swears not truly and not by God shall be whipped with rods.

He who slanders another shall be publicly denounced.

All young men shall be forbidden to play cards or dice for money or for valuable articles; but backgammon for pastime shall be permitted.

Old people may play now and then and at proper times but never for stakes higher than a *kreutzer*.

No gambling shall ever take place in public.

One day in every week shall be set apart for dancing, which shall take place in public for three hours after dinner. Men and women shall dance together. No married man shall dance with his cousin or wife.

Decency shall prevail in all mimicries, rompings, singing and whistling. No vulgarity shall be permitted, because these sports should serve as pastimes and not as occasions for loose revelry.

All such recreations shall not last longer than three hours.

All people may marry with each other freely and without hindrance, except when they are forbidden by the law of Moses on account of blood-relationship.

All priests must have either lawful wives or none at all.

In each city, three hundred men shall sit as a court, over which the count, not the burgomaster, shall preside.

In every manor, fifteen men shall sit in council with the baron as chairman.

All deceit shall be rooted out.

No merchants' association shall contain more than three members.

Wine, not made from grapes grown in our land, shall not be sold in our markets.

Cloth made in foreign lands shall not be sold in our markets.

Foreign fruits shall not be sold in our markets, except those that are absolutely necessary for our use.

All kinds of food and drink shall be allowed to all people at all times, and no monk or priest shall have a right to interfere. Fasting shall take place according to religious regulations.

All game, fowl and fish shall be common to all who desire to procure them.

Wood shall be common to all, but it must not be wasted.

As much bread shall be sold for a *helblin* as a strong man can eat at one meal.

A measure of wine shall cost one *kreutzer*. A measure shall contain as much wine as two people drinking moderately can consume at one meal.

No beggars shall be permitted in our land.

Each person shall give to the poor as much as he is prompted by the Spirit of the Lord. Charity shall be dispensed on holidays and in the churches. If the collection be not sufficient, then the balance shall be supplied from the city's treasury.

The bailiffs, counts, and all the other high officials shall show the greatest consideration to the poor.

The priests shall not be entrusted with the care of the poor, because they are unfaithful to them and lie when it suits their interests. From this source has come all the wealth which the monks and priests possess. The poor were entrusted to their care, but they proved faithless shepherds.

All those that need charity must carry about their persons a document to that effect.

Above all things, there must not be any useless labor in our land. Yet we should be careful not to destroy useful labor; if we do, there will be more masters than servants.

No labor shall be deemed more honorable than agriculture or blacksmithing.

No war shall be declared without the advice of the princes of our country.

No one shall carry about him fire-arms that are used in war.

During war time the nobles and captains shall be on the field of battle.

All women and children shall be protected.

Agriculture shall not be hindered by war.

Farmers and priests shall not be required to enlist in the army.

When war is declared, each manor shall send along a priest with the army. When the battle is about to begin, the priests shall come to the front, fall on their knees and beg for a merciful peace.

No war shall be waged for the purpose of extending territory.

No burning of houses shall be permitted.

No churches shall be harmed or robbed during war-time. Anyone doing so shall suffer death.

No peasant or non-noble shall live in a castle; only the noble shall be permitted to do so.

Henceforth no castle shall be destroyed; no new ones shall be built but the old ones shall be renovated.

In all cities every craft shall have its own quarter.

No excessively expensive houses shall be built, except those for public use, as town halls, stores, baths, schools, and places of amusement.

The cities shall build wide streets.

There shall be separate baths for men and for women.

All bathing places shall have both sweating and water baths.

All men shall wear long beards. No man shall have a smooth face like a woman. It shall be considered shameful not to wear a beard. Everybody shall wear short, unbraided hair.

All children, male and female, shall be sent to school at the age of three, and kept there till the age of eight.

The schools shall be supported from the common treasury of the community.

The children shall be taught the Christian laws from the Gospels and from St. Paul.

They shall also be taught how to read and understand both Latin and German; but little time shall be given to Greek and Hebrew.

When a child reaches the age of eight, he should be taught a trade, or else be allowed to continue his studies.

No property-owning burgher shall be allowed to live on any manor unless he is acquainted with its laws and customs.

All old imperial and priestly laws shall be declared null and void.

The common law should be known to all because everyone knows what is reasonable and what is not.

There shall be no jurists or advocates. He who cannot speak for himself may ask a fellow-citizen to appear for him.

No one shall be put under the ban for ordinary faults. Only in cases when a man publicly and persistently breaks God's commands shall the priest punish him in this manner.

He who publishes or buys indulgences shall be publicly punished. There shall be a higher indulgence; namely, to do good to your neighbor and forgive your enemy.

In the entire empire there shall be but one coinage. Every coin shall have its legal weight and value.

No priest shall be a member of any council of princes, cities or manors.

Anyone who does not keep a promise solemnly made, or breaks his oath, shall be publicly disgraced.

He who delays returning a borrowed article shall be compelled to refund the value of the article when it was loaned.

He who has plenty and yet does not wish to aid his neighbor shall be publicly punished.

He who takes interest on money which is loaned shall be lashed with reeds.

He who does not pay his debts when they are due shall be publicly punished.

A thief shall be a public servant for a year. He shall assist in all kinds of government work and both his feet shall be chained.

A murderer shall be executed.

A highwayman shall be compelled to serve the community all his lifetime.

Anyone who is observed spending more than he can afford shall be reported to his superiors.

All wasteful expenditure shall be prevented so that many spendthrifts may not voluntarily become poor men.

No servant shall be given wine until he is thirty years old. No servant shall leave his master, even when he is dissatisfied. No master shall curse or strike his servant and vice versa. No master shall pay his servant before his time of service has expired. When his pay is due, he shall be paid in cash. The master shall support and care for a sick servant for a period of two months without charge.

All cloths shall have solid colors, but there shall be different colors for men and women. Clothes should modestly cover the bodies of both sexes. Women shall be tastefully but modestly clad.

During every month there shall be a joyful public holiday in which the authorities of each town shall interest themselves.

No pastime shall last longer than half a day. No recreation

shall necessitate much spending. All children shall be taught to play a string instrument. They shall also be taught to know the common plants and the simple remedies against ordinary sickness. A well-known physician shall also be employed and be paid from the common fund, to which every man shall contribute.

No form of punishment shall be allowed that is not sanctioned by the laws of Moses, because man should not punish more severely than God has commanded.

If any wayfarer is able to explain his presence by showing papers from his lord, he shall be treated kindly by all men. If he has no means of support he shall be invited to the hospital where a citizen shall take special care of him and show him marked respect and kindness.

Idleness shall be prohibited by severe penalties. Every man shall labor in the trade of his choice. Idleness shall be considered a public shame.

Whoever gives money for masses, confessions or burial; whoever prays during the seven days or gives charity to a mendicant friar who puts away his ordinary dress and walks around like a different being; whoever honors a priest more than a baliff or councilor shall be publicly punished.

Whoever harms a priest shall receive the same punishment as he who harms a bailiff.

Unbelievers who desire to live amongst us shall not be ill-treated but shall be received as kindly as our own citizens. Nevertheless they shall not be accorded civic honors, nor shall they be permitted to revile our laws and religion.

No one shall be considered a heretic who upholds the Gospel as commonly interpreted in our country.

Scholars, priests and country people, as well as knights, shall commonly decide on matters pertaining to the wisdom and laws of the Gospel.

All burghers having property worth less than a hundred gulden shall contribute nothing to the public treasury; but those having a hundred gulden or more shall contribute a *heller* a week, which shall be collected weekly.

The above constitution, taken from Wolfaria, we would recommend to the inhabitants of every manor. When it is finally ratified by the people, and put into force after being accepted by our assembly, those who disobey it will be punished and those who obey, rewarded.

Dated in our capital city of *Wolffeck* in the month of *Gutwyle,* in the year when the cowls of the mendicant friars turn to dust.

IV

A Divine Evangelical Reformation, by Hipler
(1525)

Introduction

EVERY uprising of the common people has attracted the help and sympathy of individuals from the upper classes; the Peasants' Revolt was no exception. Götz von Berlichingen and Florian Geyer, two knights, became the military chiefs of the peasants. Wendel Hipler, former chancellor of the Count of Hohenlohe, and Frederick Weigand, former steward of the Elector of Mainz, became their intellectual leaders. Hipler was made administrator-in-chief of the Franconian bands, in which position he was of great service to the cause. His birth, associations, and experience put him in a class apart from the other leaders. Unlike them, he was a man of large views whose outlook was national not local. "Hipler was a rare man and writer, such as one seldom finds in councils," said Götz von Berlichingen in his autobiography.[1]

Hipler's main idea was to unite the various peasant bodies into one organization. With this in view, he sent around circulars calling for a parliament representing all classes of the people, to meet at Heilbronn, June 1, 1525 to consider "good ordinances, the establishment of the

---
[1] *Lebensbeschreibung*, p. 208.

Word of God, peace and justice, and also especially to confer about the ruling powers."[1] To this parliament, which was destined never to take place, Hipler proposed to present his plan of reform.

This plan, known as the "Divine Evangelical Reformation," represents the labors of both Hipler and Weigand. Its basis is undoubtedly the Reformation of Emperor Frederick III and its importance is in the fact that it proposes amelioration instead of revolution. Primarily, it is a lower middle-class document representing the interests of the small tradesman and craftsman in the town and the small landowner in the country. Hipler pays no attention to the town proletariat or to the country serf.

The emphasis in the scheme is laid on political rather than on economic reform. The administrative changes demanded in the courts, coinage, weights and taxation, are always in the interest of simplicity and uniformity, and voiced particularly the desires of the townspeople. Articles II, VI and IX aim distinctly to strengthen the emperor at the expense of the feudal estates. Naturally the princes, nobles and clergy were bitterly opposed to the scheme, as it proposed to make the first merely powerful subjects of the emperor and not independent monarchs, to abolish all the feudal privileges of the second and to confiscate the endowments of the last.[2]

[1] Fries, *Bauernkrieg in Ostfranken*, i, p. 294; Bensen, *Gesch. des Bauernk. in Ostf.*, p. 342.
[2] The plan, issued by Hipler in 1525, is to be found in Oechsle, pp. 163 *et seq.*, from which the following translation is made.

[TEXT]

A Reform Constitution is hereby ordained and presented to all Christians concerning their Needs, Happiness and Welfare.

I All priests shall be reformed and maintained according to their needs, without reference to their birth or standing, whether they are great bishops, provosts, deacons, abbots, monks, nuns or ordinary priests. Each community shall provide a good shepherd who shall earnestly teach his flock the Word of God only. The community shall have the power to appoint and remove its pastor. The latter shall set a good example to his people as did Christ our Deliverer. The priests shall be honorably supported, but what is left of the ecclesiastical funds shall go to the poor or to the common treasury.

II All princes, counts, barons and knights shall be reformed, so that the poor man shall no longer suffer oppression which is contrary to Christian freedom. The nobles should be compelled to perform their duty, each according to his rank. They shall serve faithfully their suzerain the emperor, protect the law-abiding, the widows and orphans, punish the lawless and wicked; finally, before all else, they shall protect and defend God's Word and Divine Justice.

III All cities, communes and districts shall be re-organized and reformed according to divine and natural righteousness and Christian freedom, so that human fabrications, whether old or new, shall no longer be invented. Selfishness shall be rooted out, and the rich as well as the poor shall be helped, in order that brotherly union may be brought about. All land taxes shall be at the rate of one penny for every twenty invested.

IV No doctors of civil or canon law shall be permitted to sit in the council of a prince; neither shall they be permitted to hold court; they shall be driven out, since they are not faithful servants of justice but merely paid hirelings. For ten years they have twisted the law to serve their own selfish ends. In order not to suppress entirely the Roman law, each university shall maintain three doctors who shall give advice when asked, but who shall have no power to enforce their decisions.

V It would be well that no priest, high or low, should be a member of any secular council, imperial, princely or communal, because worldly affairs darken God's wisdom and lead to laxness in God's service. No priest shall be appointed to any secular office, because worldly honors and pride will prevent his serving God. Through the interference of the clergy in secular affairs, the laity high and low have become the servants of the priesthood. The monks have taken possession of the goods of both noble and commoner. What is sinful to us is right for them and what is forbidden them, as marriage, is right for us. This state of affairs ought to be changed.

VI It would be well to abolish all worldly laws and, in their place, enact divine and natural ones, so that the poor may have as good a chance to get justice as the rich and powerful. A high court shall be organized called the *Kammergericht,* consisting of sixteen honorable men, composed of two princes, two counts or barons, two knights, three representatives from the imperial cities, three from the cities whose lords are princes and four from all the communes. It should be noticed that the nobility have only six members, whereas the cities and communes have ten. One of their number who is not a count or baron, and surely not a prince, shall be chosen chairman. Below the *Kammergericht* there shall be four *Hofgerichte;* and below these, sixteen *Landgerichte;* and the lowest courts shall consist of sixty-four *Freigerichte.* Each of these courts shall have sixteen members, the majority of whom shall come from the burghers and peasants. In the *Landgerichte* only, shall the noble and non-noble each have eight members. In the *Freigerichte,* eight shall come from the cities, four from the nobility and four from the communes. Appeals may be taken from the local city and country courts to the *Freigerichte,* but only in cases involving more than ten gulden. Appeals may be taken from the *Freigerichte* to the *Landgerichte,* but only in cases of more than a hundred gulden; from the *Landgerichte* to the *Hofgerichte* in those involving more than a thousand gulden, and to the *Kammergericht* in those involving more than ten thousand gulden.

VII It would be well that all revenues, transit duties, licenses, fruit dues, taxes and exactions should be abolished. We are so burdened with taxes that all dealing in merchandise becomes difficult and the common man has to pay higher prices. Only those taxes should be allowed that are needed to maintain the bridges, roads and passes. If any money is left over, it shall be put aside for the common man.

VIII All roads in the German Nation shall be kept free and passage over them unhindered. The prince, in whose territory violence is done, shall make full recompense to the persons harmed. All excises on wine, beer and mead shall be abolished; and they shall not again be taxed, except in cases of necessity.

IX All imposts and tribute money shall be abolished. Taxes shall be paid only to the emperor once in ten years, for God has commanded us in St. Matthew, "Render unto Caesar what is Caesar's."

X All gold and silver coins shall be melted and new ones of uniform weight and design struck in their place. All mines of gold, silver, quicksilver, copper, lead or other metals shall, without exception, be made free of taxation. Hence there will be an advantage in taking these metals from the mines to the imperial chamber, where they will be weighed and paid for. Many new issuers of coin have lately arisen, through whose activity the good old coins have disappeared; and in their place are others which are not worth their face value. Whosoever has not a legal right to coin money freely shall be prevented from doing so. All those who have such a right shall not be deprived of this privilege; but henceforth all coins must bear the imperial eagle on one side and the coat-of-arms of the issuer on the other. Twenty or twenty-one mints are sufficient for the needs of the empire. All persons empowered to coin money shall take an oath to issue honest coins so that the common man may not be betrayed. The coinage shall be regulated according to the demands of the country and of trade. Sixty-four *kreutzers* shall equal in value a *gulden*. All coins shall everywhere be of the same quality and bear the same stamp.

XI The great harm done to the poor in buying and selling commands our attention. Everywhere in the empire there shall be one measure, yard-stick or tun, in order to insure correct weight and uniform measures.

XII All merchants' associations such as the Fuggers, Hochstätters, Welsers and others shall be abolished, because through them both rich and poor are burdened in all things. No association or single merchant shall do business for more than ten thousand gulden. Whoever is found guilty of violating this law shall forfeit his invested capital and one half of the amount beyond the prescribed limit. If a merchant has more than ten thousand gulden he should in Christian fashion help others by lending it out. He may also deposit his surplus with the council of his city at four per cent interest; and the councilors may lend it to associations of poor people at five per cent, so 'that some capable poor men may get a chance to make a livelihood. All dealing in money (exchange) shall be prohibited under the severest penalties. To favor small dealers, a law should be passed applicable to the great wholesale merchants who deal in more than one sort of article. All merchants shall sell only in small quantities and deal only in one commodity.

Henceforth, no noble shall be a vassal of any clerical prince or prelate, and all estates held in fee from a lord who is a cleric shall be declared free. Secular vassals shall have secular lords who must not overburden the former with dues which they cannot bear. When a lord refuses to protect his vassal, the latter and his descendants shall be entirely free from him.

Finally, all organizations of princes shall be abolished; the emperor alone shall give protection. All agreements among the princes contrary to the above shall be declared null and void and shall never be made in the future, on the pain of forfeiture of all privileges, dues and regalia. Everyone in the empire, including strangers, shall travel in safety, whether on horse or foot, by carriage or by water. He shall not be subject to tolls or burdens and his life and property must be protected in order to advance the interest of the common man and the common welfare. Amen.

V

The Twelve Articles (1525)

Introduction

It is impossible to over-estimate the importance and influence of the famous pamphlet known as the Twelve Articles as a historic source for the economic condition of the German peasant at the end of the Middle Ages. All authorities agree that the Twelve Articles form the best exposition of the ideas and demands of the entire German peasantry, in spite of the fact that its authorship is still a matter of doubt. The rapidity with which the document was circulated throughout the empire attested its popularity. There is hardly an archive in all Germany that does not contain an original copy, often in manuscript.[1]

Many editions of the pamphlet bearing the same or similar titles and not always agreeing in phraseology appeared in the early part of 1525.[2] The exact date of the first edition is not definitely known; but it is quite certain that printed copies were sold in the market place of the city of Ulm by March, 1525.[3]

The question of the priority of the several editions,

---

[1] For Swabia, see Oechsle, pp. 246 *et seq.*; Franconia: Bensen, pp. 66 *et seq.*; Thuringia: Förstemann, *Neues Urkundenbuch*, i, pp. 77 *et seq.*; Breisgau: H. Schreiber, *Der deutsche Bauernkrieg*, pp. 197 *et seq.*

[2] For full account of the various editions see Stern, *Über die Zwölf Artikel der Bauern*, etc., pp. 149-151; Götze in *Historische Vierteljahrschrift*, vol. v, pp. 1-33; Panzer, nos. 2704-2709.

[3] Vogt, *Die bayerische Politik im Bauernkrieg*, p. 49; Zimmerman, ii, pp. 99-105; Jörg, p. 182.

which are generally undated, has had much to do with the problem of its authorship. In the Bavarian Reichsarchiv at Munich, Jörg found a copy which was drawn up by the peasants of Oberdorf. He identified as the author a certain Johannes Fuchssteiner, the former chancellor of the exiled Duke Ulrich of Würtemberg. Fuchssteiner had become a leader of the peasants largely with the idea of gaining their help in order to restore Duke Ulrich to his dominions. He soon made himself a prominent advocate of the peasants' cause in the imperial city of Kaufbeuren in South Germany.[1] The entire basis of Jörg's theory rests upon a sentence contained in the instructions sent out by the leaders of the Swabian peasants; namely, "We consider Chancellor Fuchssteiner of Kaufbeuren responsible for nearly all the articles."[2] This, after all, is only an unsupported statement of a mere supposition. Stern, the foremost authority on the subject, does not consider it possible that an adventurer in the service of Duke Ulrich, like Fuchssteiner, could have been the author of a document so full of hostility to the interests of the lords and princes.[3]

Cornelius found a pamphlet in the archives of the city of Memmingen which so closely resembled the famous manifesto of the peasants that the priority of the latter was questioned. It bore no date, but according to the opinion of the finder, it was printed about February 24, 1525. He further concluded that the Memingen Articles were drawn up by Christopher Schappeler at a peasant conference held at Memmingen and became the immediate source of the Twelve Articles.[4] It is un-

[1] Jörg, pp. 172–185.   [2] Stern, p. 54.   [3] *Ibid.*, p. 53.
[4] Cornelius, "Studien zur Geschichte des Bauernkriegs" in *Abhand. der bay. Akademie der Wissen.*, vol. ix, pp. 143 *et seq.* See also Egelhaaf, i, p. 569; Götze in *Histor. Viertelj.*, vol. iv.

doubtedly true that the former was used by those responsible for the latter, although there are a few differences between the two documents. In the Memmingen edition, the heriot and use of forest lands are not mentioned at all. In the articles on tithes, the Twelve Articles demand the abolition of the small tithe only, whereas the Memmingen Articles demand the abolition of all kinds of tithes.

Cornelius's theory that Schappeler was the author, or, at any rate, the direct inspirer of the Twelve Articles, has held its ground well down to this day. Christopher Schappeler, a Swiss from the canton of St. Gall, became an enthusiastic preacher of Lutheran doctrines in Memmingen, where he lived during the entire period of the Peasants' Revolt. Cornelius bases his view on several contemporary chronicles. Herolt's chronicle of the town of Schwabish Hall says that "one called Schapler composed twelve articles concerning Christian freedom."[2] Johan Carion, in his chronicle, written in 1532, declares that "one called Schapler composed twelve articles called 'On Christian Freedom' that nobody should pay taxes. . . . Because of this, great riots ensued."[3] The Memmingen chronicler Kimpel writes "Schappeler also composed twelve articles called 'On Christian Freedom,' that the government should not be paid any taxes."[4] This evidence is too indefinite to warrant positive conclusions; moreover, the extracts above quoted read very much alike, and one may have been copied from the other. It must be stated, however, that the career of Schappeler was almost entirely identified with religious agitation;

---

[1] Cornelius, pp. 180-183.
[2] Lehnert, *Studien zur Geschichte der Zwölf Artikel vom jahre 1525*, p. 69.
[3] Stern, p. 17.   [4] Lehnert, p. 70.

and he was never known to have interested himself in matters purely secular.¹ An entirely new theory of authorship was presented by Alfred Stern in his study on the origin of the Twelve Articles. According to him, the real author was Balthasar Hubmaier, an Anabaptist living at Waldshut, a city near the Swiss border. Stern's reasons were that among the papers found in Hubmaier's possession after he had been condemned to death for taking part in the rebellion, were some that contained references to the Twelve Articles.² In his confession Hubmaier had declared that "he had received articles from peasants which he had expanded, changed and modified according to what was Christian and fair."³ Faber, a contemporary chronicler hostile to the peasant movement, wrote that " Hubmaier had drawn up an instrument for the town of Hall and other places, particularly peasant articles which have recently appeared in print."⁴ Later, Stern modified his opinion, accepting the theory that the Twelve Articles originated in upper Swabia and not in Waldshut; and that Hubmaier was not the sole author but a collaborator with others.⁵

Recently new interest has been aroused in this controversy, but without materially increasing our knowledge of the subject.⁶ It is agreed by all that the original home of the Twelve Articles was undoubtedly Upper Swabia. Very likely it was a consolidation of the demands of various groups of Swabian peasants. The un-

¹ Stern, p. 24.   ² *Ibid.*, pp. 67-89.   ³ *Ibid.*, p. 94.   ⁴ *Ibid.*, p. 89.
⁵ Stern, "Die Streitfrage über den Ursprung des Artikelbriefs und der Zwölf Artikel der Bauern," in *Forschungen zur deutschen Geschichte*, vol. xii.
⁶ See Stolze in *Hist. Zeitsch.*, vol. xci, and in *Histor. Viertelj.*, vol. viii; Götze in *Histor. Viertelj.*, vols. iv, v and vii.

known "author" was in all probability really an editor whose main function was to supply literary form and Biblical quotations in support of the demands.

The remarkable thing about the pamphlet is that, though born in the very heat of religious strife of all kinds, there is so little of the religious element in it. All that is non-secular is contained in the first article, which demands that every community be empowered to choose and dismiss its pastor. This is a decisive repudiation of the hierarchial idea. The religious phraseology employed, and the constant appeal to the Bible for justification does not at all destroy the essential secular character of the Twelve Articles, because the language of controversy of the day was religious. As a sign of the rising secular interests it is second only to Luther's *Appeal to the German Nobility.*

It is truly wonderful that the peasants in the white heat of rebellion could have produced a statement of their grievances, so restrained in tone and so temperate in demanding only what was plainly justifiable. The Twelve Articles are almost entirely free from the emotional outbursts of the Reformation of Emperor Sigismund or the spirit of radical defiance of Michael Geismayr. The wording is careful, clear and simple and shows great anxiety not to offend the lords or infringe their rights. Of all the plans of reform produced during that revolutionary period, this one is by far the most reasonable and conservative. The appeals for "divine justice" and "Christian freedom" are the only instances of what might be called revolutionary sentiment. The demands are strictly agrarian and are by far the best statement of the grievances of the German peasantry at the end of the Middle Ages that was produced during the Peasant Revolt.

[TEXT]

The Fundamental and Righteous Articles of the Peasants and Subjects of the Lay and Ecclesiastical Lords by whom They Consider Themselves Oppressed.[1]

Peace to the Christian reader and the grace of God through Christ:

There are many evil writings put forth of late which take occasion, on account of the assembling of the peasants, to cast scorn upon the gospel, saying, "Is this the fruit of the new teaching, that no one should obey but that all should everywhere rise in revolt, and rush together to reform, or perhaps destroy altogether, the authorities, both ecclesiastic and lay?" The articles below shall answer these godless and criminal fault-finders, and serve, in the first place, to remove the reproach from the Word of God and, in the second place, to give a Christian excuse for the disobedience or even the revolt of the entire peasantry.

In the first place the gospel is not the cause of revolt and disorder, since it is the message of Christ, the promised Messiah; the word of life, teaching only love, peace, patience and concord. Thus all who believe in Christ should learn to be loving, peaceful, long-suffering and harmonious. This is the foundation of all the articles of the peasants (as will be seen), who accept the gospel and live according to it. How then can the evil reports declare the gospel to be a cause of revolt and disobedience? That the authors of the evil reports and the enemies of the gospel oppose themselves to these demands is due not to the gospel, but to the devil, the worst enemy of the gospel, who causes this opposition by raising doubts in the minds of his followers, and thus the Word of God, which teaches love, peace and concord, is overcome.

In the second place, it is clear that the peasants demand that this gospel be taught them as a guide in life, and they ought

---

[1] This translation is based on that of Prof. J. H. Robinson in *Translations and Reprints*, vol. ii, no. 6, pp. 20 *et seq.*

not to be called disobedient or disorderly. Whether or no, God grant the peasants, earnestly wishing to live according to His Word, their requests who shall find fault with the will of the Most High? Who shall meddle in His Judgments or oppose His Majesty? Did He not hear the Children of Israel when they called upon Him and save them out of the hands of Pharaoh? Can He not save His own to-day? Yea, He will save them and that speedily. Therefore, Christian reader, read the following article with care and then judge. Here follow the articles:

I First, it is our humble petition and desire, as also our will and resolution, that in the future we shall have power and authority so that each community shall choose and appoint a pastor, and that we shall have the right to depose him should he conduct himself improperly. The pastor thus chosen should teach us the gospel pure and simple, without any additional doctrine or ordinance of man. For to teach us continually the true faith will lead us to pray God that through His grace this faith may increase within us and become part of us. For if His grace work not within us we remain flesh and blood, which availeth nothing; since the Scripture clearly teaches that only through faith can we come to God. Only through His mercy can we become holy. Hence such a guide and pastor is necessary and in this fashion grounded upon the Scriptures.

II According as the just tithe is established by the Old Testament and fulfilled in the New, we are ready and willing to pay the fair tithe of grain. The word of God plainly provides that in giving rightly to God and distributing to His people the services of a pastor are required. We desire that for the future our church provost, whomsoever the community may appoint, shall gather and distribute this tithe. From this he shall give to the pastor, elected by the whole community, a decent and sufficient maintenance for him and his, as shall seem right to the whole community. What remains over shall be given to the poor of the place, as the circumstances and the general opinion demand. Should anything farther remain, let it be kept, lest anyone should have to leave the country on account of poverty. In case one or more villages themselves have sold the tithe on account of want, and formal testimony to this effect is given by an entire village, the claims of those to collect this tithe shall not be considered valid; but we will, as behooves us, make an agreement with such claimants to the end that we may repay the same in due time and manner. But those who have tithes which they have not purchased from a village, but which were appropriated by their ancestors, should not, and ought not to be paid any farther by the village, which shall apply its tithes to the support of the pastors elected as above indicated, or to assist the poor as is taught by the Scriptures. The small tithes,[1] whether ecclesiastical or lay, we will not pay at all, for the Lord God created cattle for the free use of man. We will not, therefore, pay farther an unseemly tithe which is of man's invention.

III It has been the custom hitherto for men to hold us as their own property, which is pitiable enough, considering that Christ has delivered and redeemed as all, the lowly as well as the great, without exception, by the shedding of His precious blood. Accordingly it is consistent with Scripture that we should be free and should wish to be so. Not that we would wish to be absolutely free and under no authority. God does not teach us that we should lead a disorderly life in the lusts of the flesh, but that we should love the Lord our God and our neighbor. We would gladly observe all this as God has commanded us in the celebration of the communion.[2] He has not commanded us not to obey the authorities, but rather that we should be humble, not only towards those in authority, but towards every one. We are thus ready to yield obedience according to God's law to our elected and regular authorities in all proper things becoming a Christian. We therefore take it for granted that you will release us from serfdom as true

[1] *Cf. supra*, p. 48.
[2] A reference to the Gospel of John, chap. xiii.

Christians, unless it should be shown us from the Gospel that we are serfs.

IV In the fourth place, it has been the custom heretofore that no poor man should be allowed to touch venison or wild fowl, or fish in flowing water, which seems to us quite unseemly and unbrotherly as well as selfish and not agreeable to the Word of God. In some places the authorities preserve the game to our great annoyance and loss, recklessly permitting the unreasoning animals to destroy to no purpose our crops, which God suffers to grow for the use of man; and yet we must submit quietly. This is neither godly nor neighborly; for when God created man He gave him dominion over all the animals, over the birds of the air and over the fish in the water. Accordingly it is our desire, if a man holds possession of waters, that he should prove from satisfactory documents that his right has been unwittingly acquired by purchase. We do not wish to take it from him by force, but his rights should be exercised in a Christian and brotherly fashion. But whosoever cannot produce such evidence should surrender his claim with good grace.[1]

V In the fifth place, we are aggrieved in the matter of wood-cutting, for the noble folk have appropriated all the woods to themselves alone. If a poor man requires wood, he must pay double price for it. It is our opinion in regard to a wood which has fallen into the hands of a lord, whether spiritual or temporal, that unless it was duly purchased it should revert again to the community. It should moreover, be free to every member of the community to help himself to such firewood as he needs in his home. Also, if a man requires wood for carpenter's purposes he should have it free, but with the knowledge of a person appointed by the community for that purpose. Should, however, no such forest be at the disposal of the community let that which has been

---

[1] Compare above with Arts. II–IV of the decree abolishing the Feudal System in France, August, 1789. *Translations and Reprints*, vol. i, no. 5, p. 3.

duly bought be administered in a brotherly and Christian manner. If the forest, although unfairly appropriated in the first instance, was later duly sold, let the matter be adjusted in a friendly spirit and according to the Scriptures.

VI Our sixth complaint is in regard to the excessive services which are demanded of us and which are increased from day to day. We ask that this matter be properly looked into so that we shall not continue to be oppressed in this way, but that some gracious consideration be given us, since our forefathers were required only to serve according to the Word of God.

VII Seventh, we will not hereafter allow ourselves to be further oppressed by our lords, but will let them demand only what is just and proper according to the word of agreement between the lord and the peasant. The lord should no longer try to force more services or other dues from the peasant without payment, but should permit the peasant to enjoy his holding in peace and quiet. The peasant should, however, help the lord when it is necessary, and at proper times, when it will not be disadvantageous to the peasant, and for a suitable payment.

VIII In the eighth place, we are greatly burdened by holdings which cannot support the rent exacted from them. The peasants suffer loss in this way and are ruined; and we ask that the lords may appoint persons of honor to inspect these holdings, and fix a rent in accordance with justice, so that the peasant shall not work for nothing, since the laborer is worthy of his hire.

IX In the ninth place, we are burdened with a great evil in the constant making of new laws. We are not judged according to the offense, but sometimes with great ill-will and sometimes much too leniently. In our opinion, we should be judged according to the old written law, so that the case shall be decided according to its merits, and not with partiality.

X In the tenth place, we are aggrieved by the appropriation by individuals of meadows and fields which at one time belonged to the community. These we will take again into our own hands. It may, however, happen that the land was rightfully purchased; when, however, the land has unfortunately been purchased in this way, some brotherly arrangement should be made according to the circumstances.

XI In the eleventh place, we will entirely abolish the due called "heriot", and will no longer endure it, nor allow widows and orphans to be thus shamefully robbed against God's will, and in violation of justice and right, as has been done in many places, and by those who should shield and protect them. These lords have disgraced and despoiled us, and although they had little authority they assumed it. God will suffer this no more, and it shall be wholly done away with, and for the future no man shall be bound to give little or much.

XII In the twelfth place, it is our conclusion and final resolution that if any one or more of the articles here set forth should not be in agreement with the Word of God, as we think they are, such article we will willingly retract if it is proved really to be against the Word of God by a clear explanation of the Scripture. Or if articles should now be conceded to us that are hereafter discovered to be unjust, from that hour they shall be void and null and without force. Likewise, if more complaints should be discovered which are based upon truth and the Scriptures and relate to offenses against God and our neighbor we are determined to reserve the right to present these also, and to exercise ourselves in all Christian teaching. For this we shall pray to God, since He can grant our demands, and He alone. The peace of Christ abide with us all.

VI

A National Constitution, by Geismayr (1526)

Introduction

THE uprising in the Tyrol was of a different character from those in the other parts of the empire, because the Tyrolese were not exclusively peasants engaged in agriculture. The enclosure movement among the large landowners which limited more and more the hunting area of the district and the mine monopoly of the Fuggers were the principal causes of the revolt in the Tyrol.[1] During the latter part of the fifteenth century extraordinary prosperity prevailed among the inhabitants of this mountain province. "Tyrol is blessed with money and mines," declares a contemporary chronicle, "hence all of man's needs are satisfied and at a small cost. The miners and the other people of the district are all prosperous and contented, so that there is a common proverb, 'if an angel fell from heaven he would fall to the Tyrol.'"[2] The production of gold and silver brought adventurers from all over Europe who came to seek their fortunes. Many of these became wealthy through lucky speculation. This attracted the attention of the

---

[1] C. Höfler in *Archiv für österreich. Geschichte*, vol. xi, p. 204.
[2] Franz Schweygers Chronik der Stadt Hall, quoted by Jäger, *Beitrag zur tirolisch-salzburgischen Bergwerksgeschichte*, p. 339.

Augsburg capitalists who soon began to extend their operations in the mining districts by advancing money to the governing duke in return for concessions of mining property. In 1488 Archduke Sigismund, being in need of money to prosecute a war with Venice, gave over the control of all the silver mines in the Tyrol in return for a loan of 150,000 florins, and in 1496, all the copper mines for a loan of 121,600 florins.[1] In this way nearly all the Tryolean mines passed into the hands of the great Fugger monopoly.[2]

When, in 1525, the peasants rose all over Germany, those in the Tyrol were the first to take the field and the last to be conquered. An assembly composed of burghers and peasants met in the town of Meran where they drew up one hundred and six articles which were presented to the provincial diet at Innsbruck, June 15, 1525.[3] They asked for the complete secularization of all church property, the right of each community to choose its pastor, the right to hunt and fish, the reform of the coinage and courts, and particularly the destruction of the Fugger monopoly. Archduke Ferdinand refused to accede to these demands, with the result that the insurrection became more violent. The city of Salsburg was captured and plundered by the insurgents, and the bishop driven out. Ferdinand finally succeeded in

[1] Ehrenberg, i, p. 91; Jäger, p. 352.

[2] The popular feeling against "Fuggerei" was so strong, that in Geismayr's plan special attention is paid to the question of mine monopoly. Cf. infra, p. 156.

[3] The Tyrol was one of the few places where the peasants had equal representation with the nobles and burghers in the local assemblies. Neither serfdom nor villeinage existed there to any extent. All the peasants were freemen who paid only a nominal ground-rent for their holdings. See Janssen, i, pp. 332, 335.

suppressing the rebellion with the help of the soldiers of the Swabian league.[1]

The leader of the Tyrolese, Michael Geismayr, was one of the most extraordinary characters produced by the peasant movement. A noble by birth, and former confidential secretary and tax collector of the Bishop of Brixen, Geismayr was nevertheless a convinced revolutionist of the most radical kind, whose great object was the establishment of a Christian republic in the Tyrol. After the suppression of the revolt, he was compelled to flee to Venice where he lived for several years in lordly style, as advisor to the Venetian government. He proposed a scheme to the Venetians to attack Ferdinand's dominions by an alliance with the Swiss Protestant towns and an invasion of the Tyrol. Ferdinand, becoming aware of this, put a price on Geismayr's head, which brought about his death by assassination in 1528.[2]

For boldness and originality, the plan of reform issued by Geismayr in January, 1526, is by far the most remarkable of those produced during the peasants' revolutionary movement.[3] In both spirit and matter it must be sharply differentiated from any of the preceding schemes. As a rule, the reform ideas of the peasants do not go far beyond a demand for the abolition of particular abuses. Now for the first time we catch a gleam of a constructive policy along radical economic lines. It would not be too much to say that Geismayr's scheme, alone of all the others, shows a touch of the modern

[1] For full treatment see Bucholtz, *Geschichte des Regierung Ferdinand des Ersten*, viii, pp. 340 *et seq.;* Hirn, *Geschichte der tiroler Landtage*, 1518-1525.

[2] Bucholtz, viii, pp. 347-349; ix, pp. 655-656; Jörg, pp. 632-657.

[3] The pamphlet is printed in full in Bucholtz, ix, pp. 651-655.

spirit. His demand that regular salaries be paid to the judges by the government instead of fees by litigants, and that all local internal customs tariffs be abolished and one system of external custom duties substituted for the whole empire, are fully along modern lines. Analogous is his scheme of government asylums for the poor, sick and aged. The declaration that the government should own the mines, because private monopoly had not resulted in advancing the common welfare, is radical enough even to-day. In the demand for the abolition of all privileges the Declaration of the Rights of Man is not more drastic. Nevertheless, the mediaeval hatred of capital and the exaltation of the country above the city mar a document that could otherwise have been produced at the beginning of the nineteenth century as well as at the beginning of the sixteenth.

[TEXT]
A National Constitution.

I At the very outset you must pledge your lives and property, not to desert each other but to co-operate at all times; always to act advisedly and to be faithful and obedient to your chosen leaders. You must seek in all things, not your own welfare, but the glory of God and the commonweal, so that the Almighty, as is promised to those who obey Him, may give us His blessing and help. To Him we entrust ourselves entirely because He is incorruptible and betrays no one.

II All those godless men who persecute the Eternal Word of God, who oppress the poor and who hinder the common welfare shall be extirpated.

III The true Christian doctrines founded on the Holy Word of God shall be proclaimed, and you must zealously pledge yourselves to them.

IV All privileges shall be done away with, as they are contrary to the Word of God, and distort the law which declares that no one shall suffer for the misdeeds of others.

V All city-walls, castles and fortresses shall be demolished. From now on, cities shall cease to exist and all shall live in villages. From cities result differences in station in the sense that one deems himself higher and more important than another. From cities come dissension, pride and disturbances; whereas in the country absolute equality reigns.

VI All pictures, images and chapels that are not parish churches (which are a horror unto God and entirely unChristian) shall be totally abolished throughout the land.

VII The Word of God is to be at all times faithfully preached in the empire, and all sophistry and legal trickery shall be uprooted and all books containing such evil writings, burned.

VIII The judges, as well as the priests in the land, shall be paid only when they are employed, in order that their services may be obtained at the least expense.

IX Every year each community shall choose a judge and

eight sworn jurors who shall administer the law during that year.

X Court shall be held every Monday and all cases shall be brought to an end within two days. The judges, sworn scribes, advocates, court attendants and messengers shall not accept money from those concerned in the lawsuit, but they shall be paid by the community. Every Monday all litigants shall appear before the court, present their cases and await decision.

XI There shall be only one government in the land, which should be located at Brixen as the most suitable place, because it is in the center of the empire, and contains many monasteries and other places of importance. Hither shall come the officials from all parts of the land, including several representatives from the mines who shall be chosen for that purpose.

XII Appeals shall be taken immediately to this body and never to Meran where it is useless to go. The administration at Meran shall be forthwith abolished.

XIII At the seat of government, there shall be established a university wherein the Word of God alone shall be taught. Three learned members of this university, well versed in Holy Scriptures (from which alone the righteousness of God can be taught) shall be appointed members of the government. They shall judge all matters according to the commands of God as is proper among a Christian people.

Each province shall, after consulting with the others, decide whether the taxes are to be abolished from now on or whether a " free year " shall be established as is ordained in the Bible. In the meanwhile taxes should be collected for public purposes. We must remember that the empire will need money for carrying on war.

It is in the general interest to abolish customs tariffs in the interior, but to permit them at the frontiers; this will establish the principle of taxing imports and not exports.

Every man shall pay the tithe according to the Word of God; it shall be spent in the following manner: In each parish there shall be a priest to preach the Scriptures and he shall be supported from the tithe in a respectable fashion. The rest of the tithe shall be given to the poor; but such regulations shall be made as will do away with house-to-house begging, so that idle loafers may no longer be permitted to collect charity. The monasteries and houses of the Teutonic Knights shall be turned into asylums. In some of these, only sick people shall be housed; and they must be well cared for with food and medicines. In others, old people who can no longer work shall be maintained; and in some, poor, uneducated children shall be respectably brought up. The poor who remain at home shall be assisted on the advice of the district judge, since he is best informed. Such people shall be provided for, according to their needs, from the tithe or by charity. If the tithe be not enough for the support of the priests and the poor, then let each man loyally give charity according to his ability and any shortage shall be made up from the public treasury. One official shall do nothing else except look after the asylums and the poor. Every judge, each in his own district, shall, by means of the tithe, charity and public appeals, be helpful to the poor at their homes. They shall be provided not only with meat and drink, but with clothing and other necessities as well, so that good morals prevail in the land.

There shall be four captains and over them a chief who shall look after the military needs of the country. They shall provide passes, roads, bridges, waterways, highways and other military necessities. All proposals for improvement must be the result of inspection and investigation. These proposals must be first reported to the government and no action is to be taken unless recommended by it. They shall also have power to make arable the swamps and waste lands, so that the public welfare may not be sacrificed for the sake of a few selfish persons. The swamps near Meran and Trent shall be drained in order that more grain be produced and more cattle pastured to supply the whole country with meat. Olive trees ought to be planted and saffron cultivated. The vineyards in the valleys should be turned into farms. Southern fruits shall be planted as in Italy. Between seasons, grain shall be grown, as the country lacks it. Hence the evil smells from the swamps will disappear and the country will become healthier and more prosperous. The hill-side vineyards, in which wheat can not be planted, shall be allowed to remain as they are. In every district, at a suitable time each year, the whole community shall turn all the fields and meadows into pasture in order to improve the soil.

No one shall engage in business, and so avoid being contaminated with the sin of usury. Good regulations shall be enacted to prevent scarcity as well as to prohibit over-charging and cheating; so that all things may be sold at an honest and fair price. Let some place in the land be fixed upon (Trent, for example, on account of its central location) where all the manufactured articles shall be made. Silk, cloth, velvet and shoes shall be produced there under the supervision of an official. Whatever cannot be grown in our country, as spices, shall be imported; shops shall be opened in several appointed places where all sorts of things shall be sold. No profit is to be made, as all things are to be sold at cost. By such means will all deceit and trickery be prevented and all things be bought at their proper value. Money will remain in the country and this will be for the benefit of the common man. The official and his assistants, charged with the duty of enforcing these regulations, shall be paid fixed salaries.

A good heavy mintage, such as existed in the time of Sigismund, shall be struck and the present coins be driven out of the country. Foreign coins shall in no case be accepted at their face value but shall be tested and weighed according to our standards.

All churches and monasteries shall be deprived of their chalices and precious metals which shall be melted and coined for the common need.

Good relations shall be maintained with our neighboring countries. Transient vendors shall not be allowed to peddle; but hereafter there shall be a market in Etschland and in the valley of the Inn River. A large sum of money shall be kept on hand in case an unexpected war should come upon us. The estates of banished nobles and others shall be used to cover the cost of maintaining the courts.

All smelting houses and mines of tin, silver, copper and other metals found in the country, which belong to the nobles or to associations of foreign merchants, such as the Fuggers, Hochstätters, Baumgartners and others like them, shall be confiscated and given over to public ownership; in all justice, they have forfeited them as they have acquired the mines by unjust and cruel means. The workmen were paid their wages in bad wares and bad money, though in appearance they were given more in amount than their earnings. The prices of spices and other wares rose because of bad currency. All coiners of money who bought silver of these monopolists had to pay their arbitrary prices. This indirectly resulted to the disadvantage of the poor man who found that the rewards of his labor had decreased. All the merchants through whose hands the bad coins passed demanded still higher prices. As a result the whole world was entangled in this un-Christian usury. In such manner were the princely fortunes made which, in all fairness, should be forfeited.

There shall be a superintendent over all the mines in the country who must be re-sworn every year. He shall have power to supervise every transaction and shall permit no smelting to be done except by the government. The metals shall be bought when prices are low. The miners shall be paid their wages in cash and not in goods, in order that peace and satisfaction may exist among the workers. If the mines are worked in an orderly and systematic manner there will be enough profit from them to pay the running expenses of the government. If the income is not sufficient for this purpose, a penny tax shall be laid on all to equalize the burden. Every effort should be made, however, to get the most out of the mines. The profits of one mine should be used to open another, because, through mining, the country can get the largest income with the least labor.

This is Geismayr's constitution when he dreams in his chimney corner, and imagines himself a prince.

CHAPTER VII

Conclusion

THE resumption by the State of its natural functions, so long exercised by the Church, could not have been accomplished without giving a severe wrench to the entire mediaeval system. The Church with its vast holdings, political independence and special privileges was as much a part of the economic organization of feudal society, as the counties, duchies, baronies and other feudal estates. In the century-old struggle between the spiritual and temporal powers, the latter found a new and powerful ally at the beginning of the sixteenth century, in the rapidly rising commercial interests of the towns. If the princes encountered in the Church a political hindrance, the merchants found it no less an economic one. The financial drain on Germany, due to the exactions of the Papal Court, made greater and more onerous during the pontificate of Leo X, had to be borne to a larger extent than ever before by the business interests. Land, having fallen in value, was no longer so lucrative a source for taxation as trade. The strict usury laws sanctioned by the Church were, too, felt as an obstacle by many who now for the first time had the opportunity to invest their money with the expectation of enormous profits. Hence it is no wonder that the towns became the hotbeds of the Lutheran agitation.

There have been differences of opinion as to whether the Peasants' Revolt was the first of the modern democratic movements or only the last of the agrarian uprisings of mediaeval times. Excepting the demand for the abolition of serfdom, the peasant programs offer few if any suggestions of modern ideas. Rather is there a harking-back to the "good old times" of the thirteenth century. The introduction of Roman law, the confiscation of common holdings and the organization of great stock companies resulted undoubtedly in much harm and injustice to many innocent individuals. Nevertheless, these changes were in response to the progressive spirit of the times. The sixteenth century was shedding its mediaeval skin and society had to suffer during the process. The Peasants' Revolt, while it was revolutionary, was not necessarily progressive. The movement really exemplified that type of reactionary radicalism that always springs up in times of great social changes. Like the knights, the peasants, too, were in the main fighting a hopeless battle against the inevitable political and economic tendencies of the age.

BIBLIOGRAPHY

I. SOURCES FOR THE PERIOD.

Baumann, F. L. *Akten zur Geschichte des deutschen Bauernkriegs aus Oberschwaben.* (Freiburg, 1877).
Baumann, F. L. *Quellen zur Geschichte des Bauernkriegs aus Rotenburg an der Tauber.* (Tübingen, 1878).
Baumann, F. L. *Quellen zur Geschichte des Bauernkriegs in Oberschwaben.* (Tübingen, 1876).
Bensen, H. W. *Geschichte des Bauernkriegs in Ostfranken aus dem Quellen bearbeitet.* (Erlangen, 1840).
Brant, S. *Narrenschiff.* Edited by K. Goedeke (Leipzig, 1872).
Berlichingen, Goetz von. *Lebensbeschreibung.* (Nürnburg, 1731.)
Chroniken der deutschen Städte vom 14 bis 16 Jahrhundert. 17 vols. (Leipzig, 1862-1881).
Deutsche Reichstagsakten, Jüngere Reihe. 3 vols. (Gotha, 1901).
Förstemann, K. E. *Neues Urkundenbuch zur Geschichte der evangelischen Kirchenreformation.* (Hamburg, 1842).
Franck, S. *Weltbuch.* (Ulm, 1536).
Fries, L. *Die Geschichte des Bauernkriegs in Ostfranken.* 2 vols. (Würzburg, 1876-1883).
Gnodalius, P. *Der peürisch und protestierende krieg.* (Basel, 1573).
Greiff, E. *Tagebuch des Lucas Rem aus den Jahren 1494-1541.* (Augsburg, 1861).
Grimm, J. *Weisthümer.* 7 vols. (Göttingen, 1840).
Grimm, J. *Rechtsalterthümer.* (Göttingen, 1881).
Haarer, P. H. *Eigentliche warhafftige Beschreibung des Bauernkriegs;* in Goebel's *Beiträge zur Staatsgeschichte von Europa* (Lemgo, 1767).
Kraft, K. *Briefe und Documente aus der Zeit der Reformation.* (Elberfeld, 1875).
Krenner. *Baierische Landtagshandlungen von 1429-1513.* 11 vols. (Munich, 1804).
Lanz, K. *Correspondenz des Kaisers Carl V.* 3 vols. (Leipzig, 1844-1846).
Leodius, H. T. *Seditionis Rusticae per Sueviam;* in Marquand Freher's *Rerum Germanicarum Scriptores,* vol. iii (Argentorati, 1717).

BIBLIOGRAPHY

Liliencron, R. von. *Die historischen Volkslieder der Deutschen vom 13 bis 16 Jahrhundert*. 2 vols. (Leipzig, 1865).
Luther, M. *Werke*, Weimar, 1883 sqq.
Luther, M. *Werke*, 67 vols. (Erlangen, 1826-1868).
Luther, M. *Werke*, 24 vols., edited by J. G. Walch. (Halle, 1740-1753).
Luther, M. *Briefe*. Edited by W. M. L. de Wette (Berlin, 1825-1856).
Luther, M. *Briefwechsel*, ed. E. L. Enders. (Frankfurt-am-Main, Calw and Stuttgart, 1884 sqq.)
Melanchton, P. *Corpus Reformatorum*. Vols. 1-7. (Halis Saxonum, 1840.)
Mone, F. J. *Quellensammlung der badischen Landesgeschichte*. 3 vols. (Karlsruhe, 1848-1863).
Mühlhauser Chronik aus den Jahren 1523-26, herausgegeben von F. A. Holzhausen. (Berlin, 1845.)
Oechsle, F. F. *Beiträge zur Geschichte des Bauernkriegs in den Schwäbisch-fränkischen Grenzlanden*. (Heilbronn, 1830.)
Pirkheimer, C. *Denkwürdigkeiten aus dem Reformationszeitalter*. (Bamberg, 1852.)
Schade, O. *Satiren und Pasquille*. 3 vols. (Hannover, 1863.)
Schäfer, P. L. *Das Verhältniss der drei Geschichtschreiber des Bauernkriegs*. (Chemnitz, 1876.)
Sylvius, Aeneas. *De ritu, situ, moribus et condicione Theutonie descriptio*. (Basileae, 1571.)
Villinger Chronik von 1495 bis 1533 herausgegeben von C. Roder. (Tübingen, 1883.)
Vogt, W. *Die bayerische Politik im Bauernkrieg*. (Nördlingen, 1883.)
Vogt, W. "Die Correspondenz des schwäbischen Bundeshauptmanns Ulrich Artz." *Zeitschrift des historischen Vereins für Schwaben und Neuburg*. (1878-80-82-83.)
Wimpheling, J. *Germania*. (Strassburg, 1885.)
Zimmerische Chronik herausgegeben von K. A. Barack. 4 vols. (Tübingen, 1869.)

II. SECONDARY WORKS.

(a) GENERAL.

Bezold, F. von. *Geschichte der deutschen Reformation*. 2 vols. (Berlin, 1886.)
Egelhaaf, G. *Deutsche Geschichte im sechzehnten Jahrhundert bis zum Augsburger Religionsfrieden*. 2 vols. (Stuttgart, 1889.)
Fischer, K. *Deutsches Leben und deutsche Zustände*. (Gotha, 1884.)

Janssen, J. *Geschichte des deutschen Volkes beim Ausgang des Mittelalters.* Vols. I-III. New edition by Pastor. (Freiburg im Breisgau, 1897 *sqq.*)
Lamprecht, K. *Deutsche Geschichte.* 10 vols. (Berlin, 1891-1907.)
Lindsay, T. M. *A History of the Reformation.* 2 vols. (New York, 1906.)
Ranke, L. von. *Deutsche Geschichte im Zeitalter der Reformation.* 6 vols. (Leipzig, 1868-1890.)

(b) Economic Conditions.

Bartels, A. *Der Bauer in der deutschen Vergangenheit.* (Leipzig, 1900.)
Cunningham, W. *Western Civilization in its Economic Aspects.* Vol. ii. (Cambridge, 1904.)
Ehrenberg, R. *Das Zeitalter der Fugger.* 2 vols. (Jena, 1896.)
Falke, J. *Geschichte des deutschen Handels.* 2 vols. (Leipzig, 1859.)
Kaser, K. *Politische und soziale Bewegungen im deutschen Bürgertum zu Beginn des 16 Jahrhunderts.* (Stuttgart, 1899.)
Kluckhohn, A. "Zur Geschichte der Handelsgesellschaft und Monopole im Zeitalter der Reformation." *Historische Aufsätze.* (Hannover, 1886.)
Lamprecht, K. *Deutsches Wirtschaftsleben im Mittelalter.* 3 vols. (Leipzig, 1885-1886.)
Lamprecht, K. "Zum Verständniss der wirtschaftlichen und socialen Wandlungen in Deutschland vom 14 zum 16 Jahrhundert." *Zeitschrift für Social- und Wirtschaftsgeschichte.* Vol. I.
Mone, F. J. *Beiträge zur Geschichte der Volkswirtschaft.* (Karlsruhe, 1859.)
Schmoller, G. "Zur Geschichte der nationalökonomischen Ansichten in Deutschland während der Reformationsperiode." *Zeitschrift für die gesammte Staatswissenschaft.* Vol. XVI.
Stolze, W. "Zur Vorgeschichte des Bauernkrieges." *Staats- und socialwissenschaftliche Forschungen.* Vol. XVII.
Vogt, W. "Die Vorgeschichte des Bauernkrieges." *Verein für Reformationsgeschichte.* Vol. XX.
Wiebe, G. *Zur Geschichte der Preisrevolution des XVI und XVII Jahrhunderts.* (Leipzig, 1895.)

(c) Introduction of Roman Law.

Franklin, O. *Beiträge zur Geschichte der Reception des römischen Rechts in Deutschland.* (Hannover, 1863.)
Modderman, W. *Die Reception des römischen Rechts.* (Jena, 1875.)
Schmidt, C. A. *Die Reception des römischen Rechts in Deutschland.* (Rostock, 1868.)

BIBLIOGRAPHY

Schmidt, C. A. *Der principielle Unterschied zwischen dem römischen und germanischen Rechte.* (Rostock, 1853.)
Stintzing, R. *Geschichte der deutschen Rechtswissenschaft.* (München und Leipzig, 1880.)
Stintzing, R. *Ulrich Zasius.* (Basel, 1857.)
Stobbe, O. *Geschichte der deutschen Rechtsquellen.* 2 vols. (Braunschweig, 1864.)
Stölzel, A. *Die Entwicklung des gelehrten Richtertums in deutschen Territorien.* (Stuttgart, 1872.)
General works of Savigny, Waitz, Laband, Eichhorn, Brunner, Schroeder and Maurer.

(d) The Peasants Revolt.

Baur, A. *Deutschland in den Jahren 1517-1525.* (Ulm, 1872.)
Bax, E. B. *Social Side of the Reformation in Germany.* 3 vols. (London, 1894.)
Bebel, A. *Der deutsche Bauernkrieg.* (Braunschweig, 1876.)
Bezold, F. von. "Die armen Leute und die deutsche Literatur des späteren Mittelalters." *Historische Zeitschrift.* Vol. XLI.
Friedrich, J. *Astrologie und Reformation.* (Munich, 1864.)
Hagen, K. "Melanchton als Politiker," in *Reden und Vorträge.* (Bern, 1861.)
Hartfelder, K. *Zur Geschichte des Bauernkriegs in Südwestdeutschland.* (Stuttgart, 1884.)
Herold, R. *Der Bundschuh im Bistum Speyer von Jahre, 1502.* Greifswald, 1889.)
Jörg, J. E. *Deutschland in der Revolutionsperiode von 1522-1526.* (Freiburg, 1851.)
Kautsky, K. *Communism in Central Europe in the Time of the Reformation.* (London, 1897.)
Keller, L. *Die Reformation und die älteren Reformparteien in ihrem Zusammenhange dargestellt.* (Leipzig, 1885.)
Schreiber, H. *Der Bundschuh zu Lehen im Breisgau und der arme Konrad.* (Freiburg, 1824.)
Stern, A. *Die Socialisten der Reformationszeit.* (Berlin, 1883.)
Ulmann, H. "Das Leben des deutschen Volks bei Beginn der Neuzeit." *Verein für Reformationsgeschichte.* Vol. XLI (1893).
Zimmerman, W. *Allgemeine Geschichte des grossen Bauernkriegs.* 2 vols. (Stuttgart, 1854.)
Zollner, R. *Zur Vorgeschichte des Bauernkriegs.* (Dresden, 1872.)

(e) Martin Luther.

Boehmer, H. *Luther im Lichte der neueren Forschung.* (Leipzig, 1906.)

Evers, G. G. *Martin Luther.* 5 vols. (Mainz, 1883-1888.)
Kolde, T. *Martin Luther.* 2 vols. (Gotha, 1884-93.)
Köstlin, J. *Martin Luther, sein Leben und seine Schriften.* 2 vols. (Berlin, 1903.)
Lindsay, T. *Luther and the German Reformation.* (New York, 1900.)
Ward, F. G. *Ansichten Luthers vom Staat.* (Jena, 1898.)

III. REFORM PLANS.

(a) THE REFORMATION OF EMPEROR SIGISMUND.

Sources.

Böhm, W. *Friederich Reisers Reformation des Kaisers Sigismund.* (Leipzig, 1876.)
Goldast, M. *Collectio constitutionum imperialium.* Vol. IV. (Frankfort-a-M., 1713.)

Secondary.

Bezold, F. von. "Zur deutschen Kaisersage." *Sitzungsberichte der Münchener Akademie.* Jahrgang 1884, p. 586.
Koehne, C. "Studien zur sogenannten Reformation Kaiser Sigmunds." *Zeitschrift für Social- und Wirtschaftsgeschichte.* Vol. VI.
Werner, H. "Uber den Verfasser und den Geist der sogenanten Reformation des Kaisers Sigmund." *Historische Vierteljahrschrift.* Vol. V.

(b) THE REFORMATION OF EMPEROR FREDERICK III.

Sources.

Böhmer, G. W. *Friedrich III. Entwurf einer Magna Charta für Deutschland.* (Gottingen, 1818.)
Chmel, Joseph. *Regesta.* (Wien, 1840.)
Goldast, M. *Reichssatzungen des H. R. Reichs.* (Hanau, 1609.)
Panzer, G. W. *Annalen der älteren deutschen Literatur.* (Nördlingen, 1864.)
Potthast, A. *Bibliotheca historica medii aevi.* (Berlin, 1896.)

Secondary.

Eichorn, K. F. *Deutsche Staats- und Rechtsgeschichte.* 4 vols. (Göttingen, 1834-6.)
Fisher, E. W. *Einige Bemerkungen über die sogenannte Reformation Kaiser Friedrichs III von Jahre 1441.* (Hamburg, 1858.)
Hagen, K. *Deutschlands literarische und religiöse Verhältnisse im Reformationszeitalter.* (Frankfurt-a-M., 1868.)

Homeyer, C. G. *Monatsber. der konig. preuss. Akad. der Wissen.* (June, 1856.)

(c) EBERLIN'S PLAN.

Sources.

Ausgewählte Schriften Eberlins. *Neudrucke deutscher Litteraturwerke des 16. und 17 Jahrh.* No. 139-141; 170-172; 183-188.
Ein Sendbrief Eberlins von Günzburg. *Zeitschrift für deutsche Philologie.* (1904.)

Secondary.

Lucke, W. *Die Entstehung der 15 Bundesgenossen des Joh. Eberlin von Günzburg.* (Halle, 1902.)
Radlkofer, M. *Joh. Eberlin von Günzburg und sein Vetter Wehe von Lipheim.* (Nördlingen, 1887.)
Riggenbach, B. *Joh. Eberlin von Günzburg.* (Tübingen, 1874.)
Schmidt, J. H. *Die 15 Bundegenossen.* (Leipzig, 1900.)
Strobel. *Litterarisches Museum.* I Bd. (Altdorf, 1778.)
Werner, J. "Ein christlich-sozialer Agitator im Reformationszeitalter." *Soziales Christentum.* (1895.)

(d) HIPLER'S PLAN.

Sources.

Oechsle, F. F. *Beiträge zur Geschichte des Bauernkriegs in den Schwäbisch-fränkischen Grenzlanden.* (Heilbronn, 1830.)

Secondary.

Kluckhohn, A. "Uber das Projekt eines Bauernparlamentes zu Heilbronn." *Nachrichten von deut. Gesell. der Wissen zu Göttingen.* (1893.)

(e) THE TWELVE ARTICLES.

Secondary.

Baumann, L. L. *Die zwölf Artikel der oberschwäbischen Bauern, 1525.* (Kempten, 1896.)
Cornelius, C. A. "Studien zur Geschichte des Bauernkriegs." *Abhandlungen der historischen Klasse der könig, bayer. Akademie der Wissenschaften.* (1866.)
Götze, A. "Die Artikel der Bauern 1525." *Historische Vierteljahrschrift.* Vol. IV. (1901.)
Götze, A. "Die zwölf Artikel der Bauern 1525." *Historische Vierteljahrschrift.* Vol. V. (1902.)
Götze, A. "Zur Uberlieferung der 12 Artikel." *Historische Vierteljahrschrift.* Vol. VII. (1904.)

Lehnert, K. *Studien zur Geschichte der zwölf Artikel vom Jahre 1525.* (Halle, 1894.)
Stern, A. *Uber die zwölf Artikel der Bauern und einige andere Aktenstücke aus der Bewegung von 1525.* (Leipzig, 1868.)
Stern, A. "Die Streitfrage uber den Ursprung der Artikelbriefs und der zwölf Artikel der Bauern." *Forschungen zur deutschen Geschichte.* Vol. XII. (1872.)
Stolze, W. "Die 12 Artikel von 1525 und ihr Verfasser." *Historische Zeitschrift.* Vol. XCI. (1903.)
Stolze, W. "Zur Geschichte der 12 Artikel von 1525." *Historische Vierteljahrschrift.* Vol. VIII. (1905.)

(f) GEISMAYR'S PLAN.

Sources.

Franz Schweygers *Chronik der Stadt Hall,* herausgegeben von D. Schönherr. (Innsbruck, 1867.)
Leist, F. *Quellenbeiträge zur Geschichte des Bauernaufruhrs in Salzburg 1525 bis 1526.* (Salzburg, 1888.)

Secondary.

Bucholtz, F. B. *Geschichte der Regierung Ferdinand des Ersten.* 9 vols. (Wien, 1831-38.)
Egger, J. *Geschichte Tirols von den ältesten Zeiten bis in die Neuzeit.* (Innsbruck, 1872-80.)
Hirn, F. *Geschichte der tiroler Landtage 1518-25; Erläuterungen und ergänzungen zu Janssens Geschichte des deutschen Volks.* Vol. IV. (Freiburg, 1905.)
Jäger, A. "Beitrag zur tirolisch-salzburgischen Bergwerksgeschichte." *Archiv für österreichische Geschichte.* Vol. IV. (1875.)

www.ingramcontent.com/pod-product-compliance
Lightning Source LLC
Chambersburg PA
CBHW070445090426
42735CB00012B/2465